HOW TO RUN
Successful High-Tech Project-Based Organizations

For a listing of recent titles in the *Artech House Computing Library*, please turn to the back of this book.

HOW TO RUN
Successful High-Tech Project-Based Organizations

FERGUS O'CONNELL

Artech House
Boston • London

Library of Congress Cataloging-in-Publication Data
O'Connell, Fergus.
   How to run successful high-tech project-based organizations / Fergus O'Connell.
      p.   cm. — (Artech House computing library)
   Includes bibliographical references and index.
   ISBN 1-58053-010-9 (alk. paper)
   1. High technology industries—Management   2. Industrial project management.   I. Title.   II. Series.
   HD62.37.028   1999
   620'.0068—dc21   99-41776
                                                             CIP

British Library Cataloguing in Publication Data
O'Connell, Fergus
   How to run successful high-tech project-based organizations.— (Artech House computing library)
   1. Industrial project management
   I. Title
   658.4'04
   ISBN 1-58053-010-9

Cover and text design by Darrell Judd

International Standard Book Number: 1-58053-010-9
Library of Congress Catalog Card Number: 99-41776

10 9 8 7 6 5 4 3

To Bernadette, a natural businesswoman; Hugh, a born project manager; and Ferga, who in the first year of her small life probably attended more meetings than any of us.

Contents

Preface

Six years ago, Prentice Hall published my book, *How To Run Successful Projects*. The book described a method—called structured project management—for running projects in any discipline. The book went on to a second edition, entitled *How To Run Successful Projects II—The Silver Bullet*, and continues to sell, with the twice-yearly royalty checks helping to clear credit card bills run up by shopping at amazon.com.

In parallel with the book, in 1992 I started a one-man training and consulting company—ETP, or "Eyes on the Prize." Happily—and hence the reason I can shop at amazon.com—the venture (project!) worked out, and today ETP is a thriving company whose offices in a number of locations around the globe have undertaken project management training or consulting assignments on six continents. Readers of my last book will remember a certain fondness for polar exploration, and I remain open to an offer to come and teach structured project management to any nation's Antarctic base.

The project management we teach and consult in is less about PERT (program evaluation and review technique) charts and Gantt charts and more about behavior change. Everything we do has one aim in mind: to cause the mud to stick, as somebody once elegantly described it. To make people *do* the things we teach—not just to understand them or think they're neat but to *do* them and continue to *do* them, particularly when the environment within which they operate is constantly trying to tempt them to stray from the true path.

We have had some spectacular successes—people saying that we changed their lives. Almost without exception, we got tremendously positive feedback to the ideas we passed on. Deep down, however, we wondered: Too many people were going back to organizations where—for want of a better expression—the "system" overwhelmed them. Back in their organizations—for whatever reason—nothing much changed, and whatever good intentions they had when they left our training course evaporated, more or less quickly, once they got back in the trenches.

Sure, the people needed to change, but even more than the people, their *organizations* needed to change. That is what this book is about. It takes the tools of structured project management and turns them on organizations.

If organizations do the things described in this book they will accomplish the following:

- Increase customer satisfaction;

- Shorten time to market;

- Gain market edge;

- Cut costs;

- Increase revenue;

- Increase profits;

- Enhance employee happiness;

- Make life easier for everybody connected with the organization.

Better yet, they will meet all these goals at no cost.

Acknowledgments

As always, the ideas come from everywhere, and it sometimes seems my job is merely to put some shape on them and write them down. I want first of all to thank Theo Meijer, Bernard Krack, Marc Detail, and Daniel Jung at the Goodyear Technical Center in Luxembourg. Goodyear is at the forefront of the application of good project management practice.

In addition, I would like to mention Tony McDermott of Aer Lingus; Gunnie Jacobsson of Augur Ltd.; Mike Anobile, managing director of the Localisation Industry Standards Association (LISA); Amanda O'Leary, executive director of ETP (Latin America); Fintan O'Flynn in Nortel, Galway; Terry Prone and Tom Savage of Carr Communications; Professor John Brackett of Boston University; Joc Sanders of the Centre for Software Engineering in Dublin; Olavi Hiukka at Microsoft; Paula McHugh, ETP's lawyer; and Mike Keegan of Tellabs. I also owe a deep debt of gratitude to Stephen Brown of PPP Lifetime whose red/amber/green (RAG) reporting scheme was one of the seeds from which the organization-wide status report grew.

In ETP, Sean McEvoy developed the checklist described in Chapter 4, based on Chapter 4 in my previous book. Using this as a basis, Alacoque McMenamin and Diarmaid Scully created the questionnaire in Chapter 5. They also created the concept of "projects at risk." Bernadette Coleman developed the forms in Chapter 1. Eimer Kernan pored over the galley proofs and little escaped her eagle eye.

Tim O'Mahony has been in this from the beginning, while Petra Costigan Oorthuijs was the first employee at ETP. Remember when we waited in line for the computer, Petra?

Christy O'Connell knows almost nothing about what we do, yet his advice has invariably been correct. Thanks, Christy.

Without all the other people who work at ETP, this book would, quite literally, not exist. They are enthusiastic, talented, skilled, and complex, and they share a dream; I learn from them every day. Apart from those mentioned already, they are Tom Cahill, Sandra Foy, Jackie Costigan, Trina Dunne, Hetty Murphy, Elaine Scully, Jonathan Dempsey, Ursula Watchorn, Mary Guiney, Noel Kelly, Tony O'Sullivan, Conor McCabe, Susan McHugh, Nancy Laureshan, Jim Seward, Bernadette McHugh, Geraldine Myles, Ann Dillon, Karen Molloy, Sheila Murray, Frank Byrne, Geraldine Crowther, and Rose Doyle.

If you've ever seen a world record attempt in athletics, you'll know the way pacemakers are used to push the attempt through and shepherd the runner along. The people at Artech House were my pacemakers—Mike Webb, Valerie Moliere, Sharon Horn, Susanna Taggart, Darrell Judd, and Tina Kolb. I also owe a huge debt of gratitude to Chuck Howell, who reviewed the emerging manuscript. In theory he was doing this on behalf of Artech House; in reality he was doing it for me. I don't know what they paid you Chuck, but it wasn't half enough for what you did! (By the way, the T-shirt's in the mail.) Finally, it was with great joy that I found myself working once again with Viki Williams, the best of editors and a great person.

Introduction

In this final decade of the twentieth century, projects going off the rails have become something of a cliché. (By *off the rails*, I mean projects (a) coming in late, (b) going over budget, or (c) not delivering what was required.) Everybody has his or her own favorite story; books appear from time to time devoted to the subject. The premise of my previous book was that it doesn't have to be like this. By applying a very straightforward recipe or formula—we called it structured project management, or the 10 steps—all projects can be successful.

As I mentioned in the preface, we built a business on this premise. However, about three years ago, we started to realize that we were only scratching at the surface of the problem. We were in "fix" mode. We would rescue a project here and train a group of project managers there, but how much of a difference did that make in even the medium term? For every problem we fixed, it seemed like ten bad ones sprang up to take its place.

We began to realize that a one-time "fix," while very valuable for the particular project or project manager, wasn't enough. You had to look at all the projects within a particular organization and take whatever steps were necessary to ensure that all of them became successful. If you could find a way of doing this, then it was clearly a big improvement on the previous situation.

Ultimately, though, there were still problems. There was often a discontinuity between the organization's strategic direction and the organization expressed as the sum of its projects. The whole was often a lot different than the sum of the parts.

We came to realize that by treating the organization as a project and then progressively breaking that project down into smaller and smaller projects, applying the 10 steps at each stage, we could arrive at a situation where the organization expressed as the sum of its projects was equivalent to the organization in terms of its strategic direction. This was really something because it meant that the normal overlap or falling between the cracks that exists in conventional organizational structures didn't exist in organizations that had been analyzed in this way. All kinds of good things flowed from this very precise alignment between the organization's strategic goals and the operational realities.

This then is what this book is about. We are going to take you through three levels of application of the tools of structured project management to your organization. Each level will build on the preceding ones and become progressively more beneficial to your organization, if you decide to implement it.

Level 1, described in Part One, is the "fix" level. In this level we cover the 10 steps in structured project management and how to apply them across a wide variety of project management functions. This is the level for you if you are feeling that any of the following are true:

- That there has to be a better way within your organization;

- That there appears to be no more bandwidth;

- That there is clearly financial loss and/or waste;

- That surprises on projects are the norm.

If you have already taken some steps to improve project management—training courses, for example—and you believe that those steps are starting to bite, then you can move onto Level 2, detailed in Part Two. We call it implementing structured project management in organizations (iSPMiO). This level covers the organization-wide status report and the project management performance model. Undertaking an iSPMiO program means that you have decided to make project management a key differentiator within your organization.

Ultimately, to get the most from these ideas you may want to consider running your organization as a project. Part Three (Level 3) shows you how to do this. There is also a Part Four in the book, and it describes how projects and organizations can so easily go wrong.

Finally, we need a definition to get rolling. In this book I use the word *organization* many times. When I use the word, the picture that should pop into your head should be that of your organization. If you're involved in trying to get things done, either on your own or with other people, this book is for you, whether you're any of the following:

- The CEO of a multinational conglomerate;

- The managing director or president of a small, medium, or large company;

- The head of a division or a department or a section of any such companies;

- Running your own one-person organization;

- In the public or private sector;

- Concerned with profit-making or charity.

The book is designed for either sequential reading or skimming, with—I believe—equal effect. In trying to impart information, the book uses the tell/show/involve approach—the latter, insofar as is possible with a book.

In general, each chapter consists of the following:

- Some multiple choice questions to cause the reader to think about various aspects of project management (involve);

- A spiel—I have tried to keep all the spiels relatively short, apart from Chapter 1, which is, of necessity, a bit long (tell);

- A form, template, worked example, or some other aid to assist the reader in applying the particular set of techniques outlined (show).

Finally, we would like to hear from you. Only that way will we know whether the book has made a difference *to you*. You can e-mail us at info@etpint.com. Also, many of the User Assistance items are available on our Web site at www.etpint.com.

How to Run Successful High-Tech Project-Based Organizations

PART ONE
"Fixing" Projects

In Part One, the book does the following:

- Describes the 10 steps of structured project management (Chapter 1).

We then show—in Chapters 2–11—how it is possible to use the 10 steps to accomplish a variety of project management–related functions, listed as follows:

- Scope projects and make project plans (Chapter 2);

- Run projects (Chapter 3);

- Assess project plans (Chapter 4);

- Assess projects (Chapter 5);

- Rescue projects (Chapter 6);

- Audit completed projects (Chapter 7);

- Run multiple projects (Chapter 8);

- Build a database of completed projects (Chapter 9);

- Analyze project management processes (Chapter 10);

- Manage subcontractors (Chapter 11).

In this chapter we give a brief overview of the 10 steps of structured project management. While this brief survey is good enough for government work (only joking), anyone wishing to get the complete picture should read my earlier book [1].

1 The 10 Steps

Questions

? Q.1 The "requirements complete" deadline for the project has arrived, but the requirements are not complete. If you don't start the next phase—"design"—now, then it's possible that the entire project will slip. What do you do?

(a) Hang tough and say that nobody goes anywhere until the requirements are completed and signed off.

(b) Blaze ahead and begin the design, doing those components that are based on requirements that do exist. It's early in the project—you can always make up the ground later.

(c) Blaze ahead and begin the design, modifying the schedule to include two milestones:

• Partial requirements complete;

• Full requirements complete.

In the process, however, do not alter the end date.

(d) Do as in (c) but move the end date to allow for the extra work that is going to be required.

? Q.2 The project is running to schedule, and you are near the end. The customer suddenly phones you and wants to "add just one little thing" and still get delivery as originally agreed. The "one little thing" is actually reasonably significant. You are new to the company. The customer tells you that your predecessor always accommodated such requests. What do you do?

(a) Say yes. Satisfying the customer is what it's all about.

(b) Ask the team to work some nights and weekends and have a moan with them about "bloody customers."

(c) Implement change control and try to accommodate the client's desire for the end date not to change by adding more resources. If this fails, tell the client the new end date.

(d) Use some of your contingency—assuming you have some— to satisfy the request.

? Q.3 In scoping the goal of a project, the things most likely to cause the project to fail are:

(a) Budgetary constraints.

(b) Resource constraints.

(c) Quality requirements.

(d) People issues.

Answers

Q.1
(a) 5 points: Probably the cleanest and best thing to do—even if it does require you to be a bit tough. (A bit? Okay then, very tough.)
(b) 0 points: Make the ground up later? The hell you will.
(c) 0 points: See (b).
(d) 5 points: My own preference would be for (a), but this will work too.

Q.2
(a) 0 points: No. No. No. Of course it's about satisfying the customer —but not at this price.
(b) 0 points: Or this. This is the same as (a).
(c) 5 points: Yes, and you knew it all along didn't you? You're a project manager, not a magician.
(d) 5 points: Yes, but make a bit of a deal out of it. You were able to do this for the client (i.e., save his or her bacon) because you were smart enough to put in contingency in the first place.

Q.3
(a) 0 points: No.
(b) 2 points: Sure, if you don't match demand (work to be done) with supply (people to do the work).
(c) 0 points: Not really.
(d) 5 points: Yep. There's nothing so strange as folk.

Scores

15 points: Do you really need this book?

12 points: Oops. Are slip-ups like this uncharacteristic of you?

Less than 12: You'll get yourself into lots of trouble doing things like this.

The 10 steps

Structured project management takes the view that anything can be treated as a project. Once you adopt this view, then there is a method underlying *all* successful projects. When you follow this method your project is pretty much *guaranteed* to succeed. Structured project management gives necessary (what you have to do) and sufficient (all you have to do) conditions for planning and running a successful project.

This method has 10 steps in it. Five have to do with planning the project, the other five with carrying out the plan. Each step has a score or weighting associated with it, and collectively, these weightings add up to 100. The project can be scored at any time by assigning a value to each of the weightings. By adding up the values, we get a number that we call the probability of success indicator (PSI). The PSI is an instantaneous measure of how likely or not the project is to succeed. Among other things, structured project management solves the central problem of project management (i.e., people committing to things that cannot be done—what DeMarco and Lister in *Peopleware* [2] call "gutless estimating.") It does this in the following way.

When you are given a project, we like to compare it to a missile coming directly at you. Now there are two types of missiles. The ballistic missile is picked up by your radar while it is still a good way off. You know the ballistic missile is coming when your boss says to you, "Congratulations (insert your name here), you've been chosen to lead the poison chalice project, and I'm sure it'll be a career-enhancing experience for all of us." However, there is also the cruise missile, which you know nothing about until it lands in your lap. An example of this is when you're, for example, at a meeting, and somebody suddenly turns to you and says, "When could you have that done by?"

Both of these missiles carry a warhead. In project management, however, they carry a particularly dangerous kind of warhead, which we call the "binary warhead." A binary warhead contains two relatively innocent items that, when mixed together, become deadly. These two items are the following:

- The request itself (for example, "please undertake the poison chalice project");

- The fixed constraints, or as we like to call them, the "baggage."

The baggage is the idea that even though they've asked you the question "When could that be done by?" they already know the answer! Sales has announced it for the second quarter, or there's a trade show, or there's a window in the market, or any of the other innumerable excuses people use. In our office there is a Dilbert calendar whose caption for January reads, "The boss zone—where time and logic do not apply." I'm sure you're familiar with the kind of thing I mean.

So the way this warhead works is as follows: In trying to deal with the request, you know you're going to need resources, a budget, time, and so on. On the other hand, the baggage says you don't have the resources, the budget is too small, and the time is already (1) fixed and (2) too short. You know how it goes. You want 12 highly skilled engineers, and the powers-that-be are offering you a man and a dog. If you try to deal with these two issues at once, you will almost certainly come to grief.

Structured project management deals with them *separately*. Steps 1 through 5(a) deal with the request, building a model of the project to enable you to understand what you are facing. Only after you've done that do you deal with the baggage, in step 5(b). Doing this essentially "defuses" the warhead. The steps are described in turn.

Step 1   Visualize the goal of the project (PSI contribution = 20).

More projects probably go wrong for breaching this step than any other. This step involves doing three things:

1.   Identifying the goal of the project—what lies within the scope and what lies outside it. What are the project's completion criteria, or how will we know when the project is over?

2.   Controlling changes to the goal as the project unfolds (a "change control" system).

3.   Given that a project can have lots of different endings, identifying what would be the best possible ending from the points of view of the various stakeholders.

Structured project management identifies four key parameters in connection with any project:

- What is to be delivered ("functionality");

- When it is to be delivered ("delivery date" or "elapsed time");

- Effort (or "work") that acts as a gateway into cost ("budget");

- Quality.

Tradeoffs in these will almost certainly be required to determine the eventual goal of the project.

Step 2   Make a list of jobs that need to be done (PSI contribution = 20).

Planning any project involves predicting the future. Unfortunately, in predicting the future, we will not get it right. We therefore need to do as much as we can to reduce how wrong we are.

Project management is basically the stringing together of many jobs. It is the project manager's responsibility to do this stringing together. There are three ways it can be done:

1.   It can be allowed to happen itself. This occurs when somebody doesn't devote adequate time to project management, so the project participants are left to manage themselves.

2.   It can be done in real time. This is the "fire-fighting" approach beloved by many project managers. In this approach, the project manager takes the view that not much can be predicted, that everything is going to be a surprise, and that it can only be

dealt with when it happens. If somebody uses the expression "It'll take as long as it takes," then chances are that, consciously or otherwise, this person has chosen this approach.

3. It can be done at the beginning of the project.

Step 2 holds that by planning the project in sufficient detail at the beginning of the project, many of the problems that would have occurred later can be anticipated. Where there are unknowns in the project, we can make assumptions and then build our plan on these. When the knowledge becomes available to replace the assumptions, we can then "plug" this knowledge into our plan. If this results in a change to the plan then our change control system (in step 1) will deal with it.

Furthermore, step 2 involves identifying the following:

* The list of jobs;

* The dependencies between jobs;

* The effort (or work)—*not elapsed time*—involved in each job.

The budget for each job can also be calculated here.

Step 3   There must be one leader (PSI contribution = 10).

The project must have one leader—not zero, not two, and not a committee. A good analogy for a project can be found in the old black and white westerns about cattle drives. I'm sure you know how they go. We start out on the Rio Grande with 5,000 head of longhorns, and our job is to get them to Abilene or Kansas City or some such place. The project manager's job then is to "trail-boss" the herd of jobs to the conclusion of the cattle drive. Hence, we often use the term *trail boss* to cover terms like *project manager* and *project leader*.

For a project to be regarded as having a leader or trail boss, three conditions must be satisfied.

1. The person doing the trail-bossing must take responsibility for *all* of the jobs. In general, the set of jobs breaks down into two—those being done by "our people" and those being done by the others (i.e., people in other departments, organizations, and companies). Despite the fact that the trail boss may have

no obvious leverage over these people (e.g., they don't report to him or her), it is still the trail boss's job to make sure that these jobs get done.

2. The second condition is that the trail boss must always give priority to project management tasks. Many people, in their projects, have both project management work to do and actual jobs on the project. For there to be one leader, the project management jobs must always take precedence.

3. Finally, the trail boss must be able to devote adequate time to trail-bossing.

This last condition implies that first, assuming there is such a person, then the time necessary to do the project management must be factored into the list of jobs (step 2). In the absence of any other rule of thumb, we suggest taking 8% of the total project effort (from step 2) and adding this on to cover project management. Again, as a rule of thumb, you should reckon on 0.25%–0.5% put in at the beginning of the project, with the remainder stretched out over the life of the project. If you find it more convenient to use 10% rather than 8%, you won't hear any complaints from me, on the basis that using 10% may give you a little slice of additional contingency, which is no bad thing.

Step 4   Assign people to jobs (PSI contribution = 10).

Project management is essentially a problem in supply and demand. The demand comes from step 2 where we identify the work to be done. Step 4 is where we identify the supply necessary to meet that demand. To be successful, a project's supply and demand must balance over the lifetime of the project.

There are three things you must do here:

1. Make sure every job has somebody to do it (i.e., make sure every job has a person's name on it). I fully accept that at the beginning of the project you may not know who is going to work on particular things, but—at the risk of stating the obvious—the person had better be in place before the job is due to start. Otherwise the job will be delayed.

2. Ensure that you allow for the fact that people have other commitments. For example, don't schedule people five days per

week when they are possibly involved in a second project. Also, remember that people, in general, spend a block of time every day—and all of these blocks add up!—reading e-mails or doing other forms of in-box activity.

3. Maximize the strengths of the team you've got and try to anticipate problems before they occur. For a more comprehensive discussion of people in projects, see the section titled "People" later in this chapter.

From these factors and the data in step 2, it is possible to calculate the elapsed time of each activity, the project as a whole, and hence, the critical path.

Step 5(a)   The plan must have a margin for error/fallback position [PSI contribution = 10 for this plus step 5(b)].

(This is sometimes called "contingency" or "buffer.") There are two reasons for this:

1. The plan is a prediction. Since it is a prediction it is wrong— or, to be more precise, it is not 100% right. Contingency allows for this eventuality. It allows the plan to drift somewhat from the straight line we have predicted. Provided we don't drift outside the contingency we will be okay. My colleague, Chuck Howell, is fond of saying, "All models are wrong; some are useful." This is an example of such a model.

2. Most organizations run many projects concurrently using what the jargon refers to as a "common resource pool" (i.e., one bunch of people). If all projects are running without contingency, then a slip in any of them can potentially mean a slip in *all* of them. This could happen, for example, where resources were meant to move from project A to project B but were delayed. This would now cause a delay in project B that could affect project C and so on.

Step 5(b)   Manage expectations [for PSI contribution, see step 5(a)].

By the time we have applied steps 1–5(a), we have done a really useful piece of work. We have built a supply/demand model of our project and demonstrated how it could unfold. We have a prediction, connecting the four parameters:

- What is to be delivered ("functionality");

- When it is to be delivered ("delivery date" or "elapsed time");

- Effort (or "work"), which acts as a gateway into cost ("budget");

- Quality.

We know how much the project will cost (the budget), how long it will take, what people and other resources are needed to do it, what the major pitfalls are likely to be, on what assumptions the plan is based, and a whole host of other useful information. Now we're ready to deal with the baggage. We can use the model to determine how best to do the project. We can identify different options for our management and customer. We can vary the resourcing or the budget, for instance, and see how these affect the end date. If none of our options—or "flavors" as we sometimes call them—are acceptable, we can use our model to generate other options on demand. Most important of all, however, we can use the model to ensure that we only commit to something that is actually possible and achievable. Having done this we are then in a position to start the project. (For a more comprehensive discussion about this, see the Magicians vs. Dukes of Wellington section later in this chapter.)

There are a further five steps to do with running the project (i.e., executing the plan). These are steps 6–10.

Step 6 Use an appropriate leadership style (PSI contribution = 10).
Clearly, we wouldn't, shouldn't, and don't manage all of the people involved in the project the same way. Some we know we can depend on to get the job done. Others will require lots of care and attention—"micromanagement" as the management books refer to it. This step ensures that we recognize this fact. See the People section for more on this.

Step 7 Know what's going on (PSI contribution = 10).
This step is more fancily referred to as "monitoring and control." The model we have built has served two purposes so far. It (1) enabled us to get a feeling for the scale and scope of the project we

were dealing with, and (2) it stopped us from signing up for impossible missions. In step 7 we see the third use of the model where we use it as "instrumentation" to drive the project and determine how close or how far from our original prediction events unfold ("monitoring"). Knowing this we can take appropriate action ("control").

Step 8   **Tell people what's going on (PSI contribution = 10).**
This involves reporting at an appropriate level of detail to all of the people involved with the project. At the risk of stating the obvious, it also involves being prepared to tell the bad news as well as the good!

Step 9   **Repeat steps 1–8 (PSI contribution = 0).**
We don't just plan the project once and then take a giant leap to what we hope will be the end. As the project proceeds we should constantly apply steps 1 through 8 until we eventually reach the prize.

Step 10   **The prize (PSI contribution = 0).**
Good, bad, or indifferent though our project may end up, there is one other useful thing we can do before we consign it to the archives (or the scrap heap, as the case may be!). That is to do a post-mortem on the project—or figure out what was done well so that we can do it again, and what was done badly, so that we can avoid doing it in the future. Accordingly, we should record some basic historical information (see Chapter 9) that we can then use to make our estimates more accurate the next time.

PSI

This section describes how to assign and interpret PSIs—but first a disclaimer: Despite the fact that somebody contacted me recently wanting to do a Ph.D. on the PSI, the PSI is not a piece of mathematically derived, exhaustively researched, rocket science. Rather, it is a ready-reckoner. If you imagine yourself as a project doctor, then it is your first assessment of the patient—such as pulse, temperature, and blood pressure. (If you've ever watched the TV series *ER* at all, you'll know what I mean!)

Assigning PSIs

Because of the ready-reckoner nature of the PSI, assigning values is a somewhat arbitrary process. Reference [1] gives you guidelines about how to do it as does the form at the conclusion of this chapter. The following is how I do it, and while this may seem, on first reading, to be wildly arbitrary, my experience has been that it is anything but. Using these various sources you should be able to arrive at an approach that works for you. (This is not a difficult process!)

- Step 1: This is a measure of how well-defined the goal is. Zero is not defined at all. You might get 1 or 2 for a one-sentence goal. You only get a 20 when the project is complete because only then do you know *exactly* what was achieved. Move the slider between 0 and 20.

- Step 2: This is a measure of how complete the list of jobs is. Zero is no list. You might get 2 or 3 for a high-level work breakdown structure. You only get 20 when the project is complete because only then do you know exactly what the list of jobs was. Move the slider between 0 and 20.

- Step 3: If the leader can be named and that person has adequate time available to run the project, then give 10; otherwise give 0. Reduce the 10 if the project has any kind of baroque organization structure.

- Step 4: I generally score this in the same proportion as Step 2 (e.g., a 14/20 for step 2 would give a 7/10 for step 4).

- Step 5: I generally allocate the 10 in two 5's. The first 5 is for contingency. The more contingency, the higher the score out of 5. The second 5 is for how well or badly expectations have been managed. You want to measure how closely what is happening on the project tallies with what people (i.e., stakeholders) *think* is happening on the project. An exact tally is a 5; with anything less, the score is reduced accordingly. If the project has no contingency or is an impossible mission (see the Magicians vs. Dukes of Wellington section later in this chapter), then score –15 here.

- Step 6: Move the slider between 0 and 10 based on how well the project manager varies his or her management style with the circumstances.

- Step 7: Move the slider between 0 and 10 based on how well the project manager uses the plan to steer the project. If the plan was thrown away as soon as the project was given the green light, score 0.

- Step 8: Move the slider between 0 and 10 based upon the appearance and adequacy of status reports. For a more detailed discussion on this, see Chapter 3.

- Steps 9 and 10: No score.

Interpreting PSIs

Here are the things we know about PSIs:

1. If the goal isn't right, nothing will be right. If the goal isn't right, you miss one of the two opportunities to get a high score, but notice now how it all unravels. If you don't know what you're trying to do (step 1), creating a list of jobs to do it is impossible. Thus, the list is flawed resulting in missing the *other* opportunity to get a high score. If the list is flawed then trail-bossing (step 3) is impossible, as is assigning people to the jobs (step 4). Furthermore, contingency [step 5(a)] will have no meaning; while if you don't know what you're trying to do, setting stakeholder expectations [step 5(b)] is clearly impossible. What will happen then is that everyone will set their own expectations. Since steps 6, 7, and 8 all require the job list, a flawed job list causes these to fall apart as well.

2. Forty is a threshold for the first five steps. One of the things we do a lot of is project rescues. A rescue is usually only requested when a project has gone way past its end date or wildly over-budget. Almost invariably, we find, on doing a quick PSI calculation, that the PSI for the planning steps is well below 40. This means that the project was what we call a "living dead" project. It looked like a project, smelled like a project, had all the trappings of a project—notably the consuming time, effort, resources, and money ones—but in fact, it was dead. It had no chance of success right from the outset, and all that

wasted effort could have been spared if somebody had only spotted these things sooner.

A PSI should start off low and rise steadily over the life of the project. Initially, projects may not score more than 40, and this can just mean that there is more work to be done in terms of scoping the project (step 1) and planning it (steps 2–5). However, a project should eventually go above 40 and stay above it. (Notice that the latter isn't guaranteed, and a project can drop back again. This could happen, for example, if a major change to the scope of the project went uncontrolled.)

3. Sixty is the threshold for all 10 steps. See previous comments in (2).

4. Low scores always point you at the priority problem areas, which is nice, I think you'll agree.

5. You can do anything you like on a poorly planned project and it won't make the blindest bit of difference. You may have come across Brooks' law [3]—"Adding people to a late project makes it later." Notice that Brooks' law involves two of our four parameters, effort and elapsed time. I believe that the above statement—"you can do anything you like"—can be viewed as a generalization of Brooks' law. It basically says that if your project gets into difficulties, go back and look at the plan; don't just, for example, blindly ask everyone to work harder. The problem is in the plan, not in the execution of the plan.

Magicians vs. Dukes of Wellington [step 5(b)]

Many organizations' projects fail because they were never possible in the first place. Ed Yourdon [4] calls these "death march" projects and gives plenty of advice about how to survive them. I would maintain that there is no sensible reason—including commercial or financial reasons—to undertake such projects in the first place. This section explains why I believe this to be so. It also shows you how to avoid death march projects by using the project model developed in steps 1–5.

More than anything else, not undertaking death march projects is the key to implementing structured project management in your organization. For you to buy in to this idea, however, I have to show you what you get in return.

Magicians

Projects get done because people do them. Death march projects get done because the people who do them are magicians. Magicians do magic tricks. They make impossible projects happen. If you are a magician and you work for me, I will love you to death. I will tell my friends about you. Magicians are the backbone of many organizations. A lot of organizations only exist at all because the magicians in that organization have achieved impossible things throughout the organization's history.

However, there is a problem with being a magician: If you are a magician and you work for me, then imagine me sitting in the audience while you perform your magic tricks. You pull a rabbit out of the hat, and I applaud and hoot and whistle. I nudge my friends and say, "Whoa, what a player!"

Now, unfortunately (for you, especially), the next time you go on stage, a rabbit out of a hat isn't going to impress me at all. I'll want a more spectacular trick—a dog out of the hat, a donkey, a horse, a wildebeest, an elephant, and eventually, a whale. After a while, stuff out of hats won't impress me at all, and I'll want you to go for an even more amazing trick. What's a more amazing trick? Well, sawing the lady in half is a favorite one. So now you start sawing ladies in half, and all the while I'm applauding and saying what a hell of a player you are.

One night you go on stage to saw the lady in half. You put her in the box, start the chainsaw, and imply to the audience that everything's going to be okay. Except this time, to everyone's horror, *you actually saw her in half.* Jumping out of the analogy for a moment, what happens is that the project turns out to be a disaster and blots your previously unblemished track record.

After this, something terrible happens. Every time you go on stage, you have no idea, I have no idea, the other stakeholders have no idea—the lady has no idea!—whether or not the project is going to be successful. We live in permanent suspense, agitation, and dread until the final days of the project come around, and we find out whether or not it's all worked out. Finally, if you last that long as a magician, you become that saddest of figures—a burnt-out magician. Before then though, magicians like you have usually left the organization (or worse). Then they go to some new organization where they start their magician's careers all over again.

Now, the point of all of this is that being a magician, while in itself a very laudable calling, has one monumental weakness: Like many things in the world these days, *it is unsustainable.* The longer you go on, the more and more impossible the missions you will be asked to do will become. Sooner or later you will fail. And it won't be a quiet failure. It will be a spectacular failure.

Having said all of this, however, everything I said earlier about magicians still stands. Without them, organizations would not be what they are today, but given the huge weakness of magicianship, is there any alternative? There is, and that alternative is to become a Duke of Wellington.

Dukes of Wellington

The Duke of Wellington never lost a battle. I think this may be a function of the fact that he didn't actually fight that many and that a couple that went badly for him have been classified as skirmishes. Still, give credit where credit is due. Let's go with the premise that the man never lost a battle.

He did this by painstaking and meticulous planning beforehand and then by only committing to what he could deliver. As a result, when he said something would happen, everyone believed him. His boss, the king, could take it to the bank, and the soldiers who worked for the duke could bet their lives on it.

This, then, is our proposal. Forget about being a magician, praiseworthy as that calling may be. Become a much more impressive (and rare) figure in your organization. Become a Duke of Wellington.

Objections

I can hear the objections immediately, so let's deal with some of them:

1. "In our organization deadlines are imposed on us."

    People invariably say this and they say it as though they were the victims of a mugging. They were walking down the corridor, and suddenly somebody jumped out and imposed a deadline on them. Now they may view what has just taken place as a mugging, but let me give you an alternative view.

I'm your boss, and you and I have a meeting where, from your point of view, you get mugged. I impose a deadline on you. Now look at it from my point of view. I didn't see any mugging, or if I did, you weren't the one who got mugged. I may have been forceful, I may have even used dirty tricks ("If you don't do this project then our division will be closed down" is one that was once used on me), but I see these as just part of the normal hurly-burly of management.

The mugging I see is my own mugging. I asked you to do something—albeit in a way that can vary anywhere from gentle to appalling—and you told me it could be done. If it couldn't be done, you should/would have told me.

"But, but, but," you splutter. Sorry, no buts. That's what happened. You left me with the impression that what I wanted to be done could be done. Otherwise you would have told me, wouldn't you?

"But, but, but," you splutter again (and this time you manage to get a few words out) "you gave me no choice." No, I don't think so. You always have that choice. You just didn't take it. I'm the one who has the greater right to feel aggrieved (I would maintain). You sold me a bill of goods. You lined me up to look stupid with my superiors. You put my job on the line. By this time you're drowning in your splutters. You have to admit, however, that I have a point.

2. The emperor's new clothes.

A couple of years ago I taught a workshop to a large group of people from Eastern Europe—Poland, Turkey, Greece, Croatia, and Hungary. We use a lot of analogies and anecdotes in our workshops, and some of these don't travel all that well when used in different cultures. I was trying to find an analogy to describe what happens in organizations when impossible missions are born, and I suddenly realized that the old children's story of the emperor's new clothes would do just the job.

At the risk of boring you, let me remind you of the salient points of the story. A couple of con men come to town and tell the emperor that they are high-class tailors and that if he pays them a large amount of money, they will make him the most wonderful suit of clothes that anyone has ever seen. The emperor is convinced, and he sets them up in a workshop with all the latest technology, materials, and anything else they require.

Periodically, the emperor's advisers—the chancellor and prime minister—go to visit the workshop on the emperor's instructions to see how things are going. (The emperor is engaging in a form of monitoring and control as we will describe in Chapter 3!) The two con men weave nothing on their looms, stitch nothing on their sewing machines. However, they behave as if there is the richest cloth there. They hold it this way and that in the light so that the chancellor and prime minister can get a better look at it. When the advisers return to the castle, the emperor asks how it's all going. Not wanting to appear stupid, his advisers assure him that everything's under control (to use another classic project management phrase).

The day of the big parade comes round. The con men bring up nothing to the emperor's dressing rooms. He strips naked and supposedly puts on these garments, while the con men, the courtiers, and the advisers all ooh and aah about how wonderful the emperor's new clothes are. The emperor goes out in the street, and even though he is buck naked, everybody is too afraid to say anything. Finally, it is a little child, who supposedly doesn't know any better, who points and laughs and says that the emperor has no clothes. (I can't remember exactly how the story gets wrapped up, but I think the con men make off with the loot and the child's family is made wealthy by the emperor. You probably know this anyway, but apart from the bit about the con men making off with the loot, the rest is totally untrue to life as far as being a project manager is concerned!)

Now, the point of this story is that what happened with the emperor's new clothes is exactly what happens in organizations. Somebody at a board meeting or over a lunch or sitting in adjacent cubicles (or there could be a sensible business reason!) makes some promise. This is then passed to the next layer down with phrasing such as "The board has agreed to do this on condition that it's done by blah, blah, blah." The project continues its way down the chain, borne along by phrases such as "It's cast in stone," "The drop-dead date is blah," "The window of opportunity is blah," and so on. At every point where it gets passed down to the next layer, nobody questions what has come from above. Instead everyone signs up for the impossible mission, for the death march project.

Try, however, to picture an organization where the alternative was allowed and even encouraged. (I realize fully that, depending on your organization, this could be an almost impossible feat of the imagination.) Imagine how good the alternative would be—and good not just for you, but for everyone in the organization. That is the promise that structured project management holds out to you.

3.   "Take two aspirin and call me in the morning."

Heaven forbid it should ever happen, but imagine you started to get pains in a particular part of your body. To deal with it, you decided you would go, not to your local doctor, but to a specialist in this particular area of the body. Not only did you decide on a specialist but you decided on the world's top-rated specialist in this particular area.

So imagine you went to this person and he or she said, "Yes, you've got some problems. We're going to have to take you in and do this, that, and the other."

Now imagine you said, "Ah, it's okay, doc, just give me a couple of aspirin and I'll be fine." To say the least, this would be an unusual reaction for you to have.

Then imagine, however, that the doctor said, "Okay—here you are." I think you'll agree it would be almost impossible to envision such a conversation ever happening and that if it did, then our first move, after leaving such a doctor's offices, would be to have them struck off the medical register.

Now notice that this exact conversation takes place routinely in organizations. If you are the project manager and you build a model of your project as we describe in Chapter 4, then it is no exaggeration to say that you are the world expert on your project. It is quite literally true that of all the five billion people in the world, you know more about the project, its dynamics, and how it could unfold than anyone else on planet Earth.

So you (the specialist) say, "Here's how it's going to be." Somebody who doesn't know a great deal about it tells you you're wrong, which is outrageous in itself, and then you compound the felony a thousand times by saying, "Yes, I was only joking. We'll go with what you say." If there were the project manager's equivalent of a medical register then maybe you would consider asking to have yourself removed from it, if you ever indulged in a conversation like that!

4. "This is all great stuff, but it won't work in the real world."

This is an objection that's often raised. Let's look at it. Let's say you are bidding for a project, and you build a model of the project as we have previously discussed. The model shows, among other things, that the project is going to cost $500K.

Now your customer says, "Okay, Ms. Supplier, we have a $350K budget for this project. We'd like to give it to you, but we're certainly not going to give it to you for $500K. You can have a purchase order and a deposit today, if you'll do it for $350K, and by the way, your competitors A, B, and C have all said they're prepared to do it for $350K." What do you do?

Well, you may still want the business. If you do, you clearly don't want it for financial reasons, because the evidence you have says that you are going to lose $150K on the project. However, there are often other reasons why people go after projects: The client is a prestigious one you want on your client list; the project will act as a loss leader to get you in the door to make money on subsequent projects; or the project will result in new technology that you can then sell to other people.

Having your model, you can now make a reasoned judgment of what the best thing to do is. The model doesn't stop a salesman or commercial businessman from doing anything he or she would have done previously. It does, however, give him or her better information with which to make the right decision.

I know somebody who has run a custom software house for the last 15 years. Given the world's ability to chronically underestimate software projects, it must be a cruel business. He has told me that several times in the past, they have ended up "betting the entire company" (his words, not mine) on a project (they realize now, with the benefit of hindsight). This was because they had no real idea what the project was going to cost them in the first place.

So will it work in the real world? It sure will—and a damn sight better than anything else you may have tried.

5. "If you won't do it, I'll find somebody who can."

This is essentially the same line as was used in the previous example. With a project model you can make an intelligent response to this. If the project looks vaguely within the bounds of possibility, you may decide to give it a try. If it appears wildly impossible you can just decide to walk away from it, or you can make a virtue of necessity, by saying, "Okay, it looks impossible, but we're prepared to give it a try."

We did this recently with a client. The client said it was impossible. We built a model and said that assuming certain working hours, the project might just be possible. The client, and more importantly, the client's staff, wanted to give the project a shot. They did, and it worked.

(Can I say here that I'm not going back on my earlier comments about death march projects? A death march project—my definition, not Yourdon's—is where there is no rational hope of the thing working out.)

So, in conclusion: You can be a magician, but there's no fun or future in that. Become a much rarer bird. Become a Duke of Wellington. Become a person, or employee, or organization, or company, or supplier whose commitments are considered reliable.

How do you do this? Build project models and use them to make sensible decisions on what is and isn't possible.

People (steps 4 and 6)

Projects get done because people do them. If enough of the right people do enough of the right things, then the project works out. Looking at it somewhat differently, if everybody did what we asked him or her to do, then the world would need a lot fewer project managers.

These observations are all by way of saying that it is through people—complex, unpredictable people—that we get our projects done. Structured project management deals with people in steps 4 and 6. Step 4, you may recall was "assign people to jobs," while step 6 says to "use an appropriate leadership style." These steps are important because given the amount most organizations are trying to accomplish these days, it is vital that the following occur:

- We anticipate where problems might occur (and head them off at the pass, as John Wayne might have said).

- We use our management effort to maximum effect.

Steps 4 and 6 enable us to do exactly these things.

Step 4   **Assign people to jobs.**

As we mentioned earlier in this chapter, when planning a project, we must try to maximize the strengths of the team. While there are all sorts of ways of doing this, structured project management uses the following simple and pragmatic scheme. When a person is assigned to a particular job on a project, it is necessary to recognize five situations that can occur:

1.   The person has the necessary skills and experience to do the job and likes to do it.

2.   The person has the necessary skills and experience to do the job and is prepared to do it.

3.   The person has the necessary skills and experience to do the job but is not prepared to do it.

4.   The person can be trained or instructed in doing the job.

5.   The person cannot do the job.

If part of our aim, as we said above, is to anticipate where problems might occur, then clearly they will occur with the assignments of type (3) and (5). If our aim is to maximize the strengths of the team, then we are strongest in the assignments of type (1) and (2) and weakest in those of type (4). Such an analysis can also tell us where we might best spend our training dollars. If we can move people from categories (3), (4), or (5) to categories (1) or (2), then in general that is a good thing to do.

Knowing where the people risks lie before our project begins, we are then in a position to manage these risks as the project unfolds. We manage the people risks using step 6.

Step 6   Use an appropriate leadership style.

We do this by taking the categorization scheme described in step 4 and applying the extra concept of whether or not we trust a person. "Trust," in this context, is defined to be whether we have some kind of evidence or track record that when we give the person a particular job, that job gets done. Depending on whether or not we trust the person in the particular situation we can draw up the matrix, presented in Table 1.1, showing the different types of leadership styles we should use in different circumstances. By following the scheme outlined in Table 1.1, we will indeed ensure that our limited management time and effort is used to maximum effect.

Table 1.1 Leadership Style Matrix

Person Assigned to Job	Trust	Don't Trust
(1) Can do the job and likes to do it	Consider job done	Gentle hand-holding
(2) Can do the job and is prepared to do it	Consider job done	Gentle hand-holding
(3) Can do the job and isn't prepared to do it	Problem to be solved	Resolve into a (2) or a (5)
(4) Can be trained or instructed	Watch/support them	Micromanagement
(5) Cannot do it	Problem to be solved	Resolve into a (2) or a (5)

Why projects fail

Finally, we can look at the 10 steps another way, by asking the question "Why do projects fail?" They fail, quite simply, because people violate one or more of the 10 steps. Specifically, people commit one or more of these "sins":

1. The goal of the project isn't defined properly (i.e., the goal isn't bounded, all of the stakeholders aren't identified, or stakeholders' win conditions aren't identified).

2. The goal of the project is defined properly, but then changes to it aren't controlled (i.e., there is no effective change control).

3. The project isn't planned properly (i.e., it is not planned in accordance with the principles we define in this book, notably in Chapters 1 and 2).

4. The project isn't led properly (i.e., there is no trail boss, or the trail boss doesn't fully understand his or her role or can't give the project adequate project management effort).

5. The project is planned properly but then it isn't resourced as planned (i.e., planned supply and actual supply don't tally).

6. The project is planned such that it has no contingency (i.e., everything has to go *right* on the project for it to be successful).

7. The expectations of project participants aren't managed (i.e., stakeholders are misled as to what they can expect from the project).

8. The project is planned properly but then progress against the plan is not monitored and controlled properly (i.e., we don't follow the plan we laid out).

9. Project reporting is inadequate or nonexistent.

10. When projects get into trouble, people believe the problem can be solved by some simple action (e.g., work harder, extend the deadline, add more resources).

User assistance

You can use the following form to record PSIs for your project.

PSI Record

Step	PSI Value		Deliverables From Step	Some Questions to Ask
	Max	Score		
1: Visualize the goal	20		Management summary Deliverables Completion criteria Assumptions	Have I identified all stakeholders? Are the deliverables clear? Are the completion criteria sufficiently specific?
2: Make a list of jobs to be done	20		Work breakdown structure All milestones identified Detail to first milestone	Is it up-to-date? Is it complete?
3: There must be one leader	10		One leader identified Organization chart of project	Is there clearly one leader? Is the project organization chart complete?
4: Assign people to jobs	10		All jobs have a name on them Availability of resources has been factored in Resources have been identified and level of trust established	Have I identified resource requirements? Do I know the availability of those resources?
5(a): Margin for error	10		Risk analysis Evidence of contingency	Have I identified the risks in my assumptions (step 1)?
5(b): Manage expectations			Flavors	Am I being a magician or a duke?
6: Use an appropriate leadership style	10		A winnable plan	Have I completed the category/trust analysis suggested in step 4?
7: Know what's going on	10		Tracking jobs on a daily basis	Am I doing the daily routine? (See Chapter 3) Am I able to track jobs on a daily basis? Am I opening up any "black boxes" in the future?
8: Tell people what's going on	10		Status reports issuing	Am I doing the weekly routine? (See Chapter 3) Am I issuing status reports? Is the plan being updated?

You can use the following form to assist you with tying down the goal.

Tying Down the Goal
Step 1: Visualize the Goal
The first step in structured project management is to identify your goal, your destination. Visualize what the goal is; set your eyes on the prize.   In step 1, you will learn how to clearly define and bound the goal of a project. Using what you have learned, apply this step to your own project. Write in the boxes provided the summary, goal statement, completion criteria, milestones, deliverables, assumptions, stakeholders, subgoals, and nongoals.
Management summary
Goal statement

Step 1: Visualize the Goal
Completion criteria
Milestones demonstrating definite progress towards the project goal
Deliverables

Step 1: Visualize the Goal
Customers
Other stakeholders

Step 1: Visualize the Goal
Subgoals
Nongoals

Step 1: Visualize the Goal
Assumptions

You can use the following form to help you in establishing the organization structure of the project and hence any project leadership issues.

Organization Structure and Project Leadership Worksheet
Step 3: There Must Be One Leader
The project must have one leader. It can't have no leader, and it can't have two leaders or a committee of leaders. There must be one leader and one leader only to act as the central repository of information.
In step 3 you will identify the leader of your project and identify sources of threat to that leadership. You will also complete a chart detailing the organizational structure of your project. Finally, in this step you should calculate the project management overhead (i.e., 8% of total person days).

In this project organization chart you should be able to identify the following:
   Yourself as the project leader;
   Your project sponsor;
   Your customer(s);
   Any contractor(s) or external organization on whom your project is dependent for a deliverable;
   All the members of your team;
   Anyone on whom you are dependent for a decision or a signoff;
   All likely "cattle-rustlers" (in other words those who may divert your resources onto other things).

Please fill in the following organization chart for your project.

You can use the following form to assist you in assigning jobs.

Job Assignment Worksheet
Step 4: Assign People to Jobs
In step 4 you will identify the resources needed to complete your project and the availability of those resources. You will categorize those resources according to their level of competence and motivation and the level of trust you have established with them. By assigning these resources to the jobs you have identified, you will then begin to establish the elapsed time for your project.
List your resource requirements here.
List your identified resources here.

Job ID	Person	Availability	Category	Trust		Start Date	Finish Date
				Yes	No		

Job ID	Person	Availability	Category	Trust Yes	No	Start Date	Finish Date

Job ID	Person	Availability	Category	Trust		Start Date	Finish Date
				Yes	No		

Step 5: Manage Risks

The following form will assist you in risk evaluation and management.

Risk Evaluation Form

Risk ID	Identified Risk	Probability 1–3 (H=3, M=2, L=1)	Impact 1–3 (H=3, M=2, L=1)	Exposure E = P × I	Appropriate Response

It is possible to do a lot of the work of scoping and planning projects in a relatively short space of time. Here we look at how to do that.

2 Scoping Projects and Making Plans (Steps 1–5)

Questions

? Q.1 Estimate the task "review document." The document is 30 pages, printed on one side—all text and no diagrams. There are three reviewers.

(a) 1 hour.

(b) 3 × 1.5 person-hours.

(c) One day elapsed to get it all sorted.

(d) None of the above.

? Q.2 You are a project manager and you are assigned to run an IT project. You have never before run an IT project. When you go to build the plan, the techies tell you that there is no way that they can estimate this project. "It'll take as long as it takes." Do you:

(a) Accept this.

(b) Sign up for a night course in IT and start spending all your weekends in libraries and bookstores.

(c) Insist that the project be estimated, making assumptions where necessary.

(d) Ask to be reassigned to a project in the discipline(s) in which you are proficient.

? Q.3   When estimating, who should produce the estimates?

(a) The people who are going to do the work.

(b) The project manager on his or her own.

(c) The stakeholders.

(d) The project management department.

Answers

Q.1

(a) 1 points: Doubt it. Not if the review requires individual review plus a meeting to finalize things.
(b) 2 points: Could be closer to the right answer.
(c) 2 points: Same as (b), but it's still a bit of a guess, isn't it?
(d) 5 points: First, what does "estimate" mean—effort or elapsed time? Second, what does "review" mean—individual? a meeting? individual plus a meeting? individual plus a meeting plus updates to the document? something else?

Q.2

(a) 0 points: Oh, no, no, no!
(b) 2 points: Can't hurt.
(c) 5 points: Yes, and you may have to be a bit of a hard ass to drive it through.
(d) 2 points: Okay, it'd solve the problem, but not everyone has this luxury. While you might also argue that it mightn't be a good career move, the counterargument could turn out to be equally valid.

Q.3

(a) 5 points: Yep—assuming they're available. If not, you'll have to make assumptions on their behalf.
(b) 2 points: He or she should be part of the process obviously, but not on his or her own.
(c) 2 points: Again, they should be part of the process, but not on their own.
(d) 2 points: Once again, they may have useful input, but it is the team who ultimately has to come up with the estimates.

Scores

15 points: Well done.

12 points: Okay, only one slip-up, but estimating is too serious a business for even one mistake.

Less than 12: If I were you, I'd consider very carefully the reasons why you gave the answers you did.

Introduction

One possible—and quite acceptable—way to scope and plan a project is through a sequence of meetings, drafts of documents, reviews, and so on. A much quicker way is to do it in a short brainstorming-type session. In my experience it is possible to get an awful lot done in a day, and I have never had to go beyond two days. If you decide to scope and/or plan a project this way, this chapter tells you how to do it. Incidentally, even if you decide not to do it this accelerated way, a lot of the ideas here should still be valuable to you.

The ideal precondition for such a session is that you can (1) identify and (2) get all the stakeholders together in a room. Failing that, get as many as you can, and this should still work. It just means that at the end of it, you have a selling job to do, in terms of selling the results of the session to the absent stakeholders. (Of course, you could adopt an approach that absence implies agreement! That should get them all in the room!)

Those invited can come cold, but it is better to ask everybody to put on paper their thoughts regarding the goal of the project. To get started you need the following:

- A room.

- At least one flip chart, plenty of pens, and sticky tape.

- Coffee, tea, water.

- Some food breaks.

- The stakeholders. Because terms and titles differ from one organization to another, we tend to use a general model consisting of (in no particular order) four elements—the customer, the project manager, the management, and the team. Among these you should find your stakeholders.

- A facilitator—somebody to run the session.

- A scribe—somebody to document the results. The person should have a PC and a printer and be proficient in a word processing program (e.g., Word) and a project management tool (e.g., MS Project or ETP's Silver Bullet).

Scoping the project (step 1)

The goal is your starting point. It is how you will scope the project. As we discussed in Chapter 1, you are interested in finding the ending to the project that maximizes stakeholder satisfaction. The steps in the process are described as follows.

1. The facilitator begins with questions like the following:

    - What's the goal of this project (i.e., list the various elements that go to make up the goal)?

    - How will we know when it's over?

    - What marks the day when the project is over?

    - Describe the last few activities that cause the project to complete.

    - What marks the end of the project?

    - Who are the stakeholders?

    - Can we make a complete list?

    - What marks project acceptance from the stakeholders' points of view?

    - What would be the best possible ending for each of the stakeholders in turn?

    - What's in it for the stakeholders?

    - What things lie within the scope of the project?

- What things definitely do *not* lie within the scope?

- What are the project quality measures?

- What will be the external perception of the project?

- Are there any issues to do with people that lie within the scope of the project? (If there aren't, they're lying!)

2. Note these answers down on the flip chart.

3. Tape the flip chart pages up on the wall and "play them back." Ask questions like "If we do all of this, will we have achieved the goal of the project?"

4. When you get to a point where you have a reasonable level of agreement, you've got a first cut at the scoping.

Making the plan (steps 2–5)

Now that we know what we're trying to do, we can build the plan to do it.

List of jobs

Now brainstorm to build the list of jobs, following these steps:

1. Put in "start" and "end."

2. Put in the 6–10 major milestones and/or (you can mix them at this stage) phases of the project.

3. Now, going phase by phase, begin to fill in the detailed jobs. Ask questions like these:

- Who does what?

- What happens next?

- Where does the output of the previous job go? (Do we know the output? If not, then maybe we're not clear what the job was.) Take small steps. Try to chain together all the little sequences of jobs. If somebody offers a big job, open it up to see the little jobs and how they are connected.

4. As you go along building the list of jobs, it's not too much to also expect you to capture the dependencies between jobs at this point.

Having built the list, now estimate the effort or work involved in each job (in units like, for example, person-days or person-hours). Use the following guidelines:

1. Where several estimates are offered, always take the highest one.

2. Periodically question estimates—"What's that estimate based on?" and "Why do you think it would be that?"

3. Record the basis for the estimate as well as the estimate itself.

4. If people are reluctant to estimate, either through lack of knowledge or because they are afraid of committing themselves to something, use assumptions to both replace the knowledge and reduce their insecurity. To illustrate this, please allow me a rather long digression on the power of assumptions. (See sidebar.)

5. We end up with the following:

   • A list of jobs;

   • The amount of work (also called "effort") involved in each job (and so also, the total amount of work in the project, and hence part of what is necessary to calculate the project budget);

   • The dependencies between jobs;

   • Any assumptions relevant to the job.

6. One final validation of the job list is to go back through the various elements of the goal and ensure that every element is represented in the job list. In other words, ensure that every element of the goal has jobs associated with it that result in the accomplishment of that element.

The power of assumptions

Recently we helped somebody quantify their company's year 2000 project. He started out by saying, "We have absolutely no idea. We haven't even looked at it yet, to even begin scoping it."

"Okay," we said, "let's see if we can scope it now. First question—how many systems need looking at?"

"We don't even know that much."

"Well, is it 500?"

"Oh no, don't be ridiculous, it's not 500. More like 40."

"Okay, 40. Well, let's assume 50. Next question. What has to be done to each system?"

"Well, some kind of analysis, then the actual doing of the work. And then testing it to make sure everything's okay."

"So, a sequence of three jobs—analysis, doing the work, and testing—to be carried out 50 times."

"Yep."

"Third question. Are all the systems the same?"

"No, some are enormous, old, very complex; some are small, modern, streamlined."

"So we could categorize them?"

"Sure."

"Into how many categories."

"Dunno."

"How about three—small, medium, and large?"

"Okay."

"So how many of the 50 are small?"

"Dunno."

"Approximately. Can we make some assumption?"

"Okay, say one-third of them are small."

"17?"

"Say 15."

"Medium?"

"Say 20."

"And so the other 15 are large."

"Some of them are really large."

"How many?"

"Say half a dozen."

"Okay, so assuming there are 50 systems, our second assumption is that the distribution of these systems is:

- Small: 15;

- Medium: 20;

- Large: 9;

- Very large: 6;

- Total: 50.

"Now, presumably each of our three steps—analysis, doing the work, and testing—is going to require different amounts of effort (work) depending on whether the system is small, medium, large, or very large?"

"Of course."

"And so, if we could estimate each of these three steps for each type of system, then we would have an estimate of the entire project."

"Sure would."

"Okay, so let's estimate a small one. Analysis for a small one?"

"Dunno. Maybe a week."

"Five person-days?"

"Okay, if you're going to be pedantic."

"Well, yes, I am actually."

"Okay, five person-days."

"What's that based on?"

"It's a guess."

"You mean an assumption?"

"There you go being pedantic again."

"Okay, we'll live with five person-days for now, because we're in a rush, and we just want to do a coarse estimate at this stage. But can you see—if we wanted to—that in exactly the same way that we broke down the job of 'doing' each system into three jobs (analysis, doing the work, and testing), we could break down 'analysis' further into perhaps five jobs, and by estimating each of these we would come up with a more accurate estimate than five person-days?"

"Sure."

"Okay, but for the moment let's stick with a small system, with the following figures:

- Analysis: 5;

- Doing the work: 15 (assuming three times the analysis figure);

- Testing: 10 (assuming double the analysis figure—or we might have chosen half the "do the work" figure—or anything else that sounded sensible).

"Now can we use these to determine the estimates for medium, large, and very large? We can come up with some more multipliers, can't we? Okay, so let's do it. Let's assume the following:

- Medium is three times a small.

- Large is four times a medium.

- Very large is three times a large.

"So now we can estimate the whole fandango."

	Small	Medium	Large	Very Large
Analysis	5	15	60	180
Doing the work	15	45	180	540
Testing	10	30	120	360

"But it's all just guesswork."

"But project planning is *guesswork*. What we've done here almost certainly isn't 100% right. But it's the best we're going to do at this point in the project. What we've done is we've built a model based on assumptions. You can think of the assumptions as being parameters to which we have given estimated values now, because we don't know the real ones. Knowing the real ones will make the model more accurate, but the model has a certain level of accuracy now. And we can use that to go forward. It's not ideal but we won't get any better. We absolutely won't. We call it 'counting the bricks in the wall' or 'figuring out how much stuff has to be moved.'"

One leader

Here you must do the following:

1. Identify the trail boss.

2. Calculate the project management effort (say, using the 10% of total effort rule of thumb given in Chapter 1).

    After you have done step 4 and you know the project's elapsed time, you will be able to convert this effort figure to an hours-per-day or days-per-week figure.

Assign people to jobs

This requires you to:

1. List those available to do the project.

2. Quantify their availability in terms of, say, hours per day or days per week.

3. Using this, identify how long each job will take. Do this in the following manner:

    • First by dividing work by availability to get elapsed time;

    • Then, in addition, by allowing for any public holidays or vacation days.

    Project management tools such as MS Project prove useful here, because they do these calculations (relatively!) painlessly.

4. The result of this step is that we now end up with the following:

    • A list of jobs;

    • The amount of work (also called "effort") involved in each job (and so also, the total amount of work in the project, and hence part of what is necessary to calculate the project budget);

    • The dependencies between jobs;

    • Who's going to do each job;

    • That person's availability;

- By using the amount of work figure and the availability of those doing each job, how long the job will take (the elapsed time);

- The cost of the task;

- Any assumptions relevant to the job.

Put contingency into the plan

Do the following two things here:

1. Do something like adding on extra time to the project as a whole, to each individual phase, to each item on the critical path, and/or reduce people's availability.

2. Do a simple risk analysis using a high (3), medium (2), low (1) scale. Table 2.1 provides an example.

Table 2.1 Simple Risk Analysis

	Risks	Likelihood	Impact	L x I	Action
1	Poor project management	2	3	6	Performance review Training Quality assurance Use of PSI
2	Under-resourcing	3	3	9	Verify targets against market data Advertise in January Sort dance cards
3	Managers get sick	1	2	2	
4	Over-resourcing	2	2	4	
5	Consultants get sick	2	3	6	Shadowing Medicals for new employees Sort any existing problems
6	Lack of expertise	2	3	6	Training and development Proper and timely appraisals
7	Office being in Athy	1	1	1	
8	Results (limited)	1	2	2	
9	Revenues don't happen—forecast is wrong	2	3	6	Weekly monitoring and change control Financial and management reports Difference between sales and revenue targets

Table 2.1 (continued)

	Risks	Likelihood	Impact	L x I	Action
10	Another coup	1	3	3	
11	SB flops	2	2	4	
12	Clients walk	1	3	3	
13	Unrealistic goals	2	3	6	Change control
14	Facilities blowout	3	3	9	Get Noel to concrete yard
					Get temporary offices
15	Data security	3	3	9	Discuss on 7 December
16	No head of IS	3	2	6	Advertise now
					Agree on interim solution on 7 December
17	Brand fatigue	2	2	4	
18	Competition	3	2	6	Competitive analysis
					Monthly review
					Spies
					Audits on lost customers
19	Get product management wrong	3	2	6	Define role
					Get trail boss
					Market research
20	Cash flow	2	3	6	Keep Bernie/Tim on it
21	Market changes	1	3	3	
22	Recession hits	1	3	3	
23	New market distracts management	1	3	3	

A couple of contingencies that should be considered as part of every project plan are (1) disaster recovery and (2) losing key people, or to write it in computer-speak—"a single point of failure in the liveware."

1. Disaster recovery: I wrote this book on a laptop computer. Months after it was finished I kept finding sets of backup disks around the house, in all sorts of unlikely places. I was extremely anxious about losing any of the work I had done and acted, some would say, quite paranoid as a result. A healthy paranoia is, perhaps, no bad thing. Disaster recovery is a well-trodden area, and there are a bunch of straightforward things like backups, alternate sourcing plans, off-site storage, insur-

ance, and so on that should be considered and implemented where necessary.

2. Single point of failure in the liveware: Again, a few simple steps can be taken to defend against this risk. Taking a hint from the theatrical world, we can have understudies—people who "shadow" or "buddy" other people. Every key area should have a main person and shadow who can step in, if required. Make the plan, and status reporting against the plan, more visible (i.e., so that everybody understands the big picture and his or her part in it and can also help if somebody has to hurriedly step into somebody else's shoes).

   As a result of the risk analysis step, we now end up with the following:

   - A list of jobs;
   - The amount of work (also called "effort") involved in each job (and so also, the total amount of work in the project, and hence part of what is necessary to calculate the project budget);
   - The dependencies between jobs;
   - Who's going to do each job;
   - That person's availability;
   - By using the amount of work and the availability of the person doing the job and how long the job will take (the elapsed time);
   - The cost of the task;
   - Any assumptions relevant to the job;
   - Any risk involved in the task;
   - The contingency—if any—associated with the task.

Iterate steps 2–5(a)

While you have been doing all of this, the scribe will have been busily following you, documenting all of this material and perhaps entering it into a project management tool. You now use the material the scribe has generated to see how you stand.

It may be that you don't like, for example, the end date that your plan is showing. You can now play with resources, functionality, or any of the four parameters to see if you can bring the plan more in line with the stakeholders' expectations or wishes.

Document the plan

We offer a couple of possible layouts at the conclusion of this chapter.

Present the plan

Next, the plan should be fed back to the group present. (Ultimately, it should be presented to all of those affected by the project.) Sending them a copy of the plan, while a good thing to do, is really not enough. Talk them through it, show them the big picture and their part in it, tell them what they can expect at different points in its unfolding, show them the key milestones, explain the critical path, and take them through the major risks. Even though you involved them in the planning, play the whole thing back to them. "Tell them the whole gig," as my friend, Paul McCarthy would say. Without exaggeration, a half hour spent doing this will repay itself a thousand fold. In the User Assistance section at the end of this chapter, we give some guidelines on how best to structure this presentation.

Agree on next actions

Finally, by consulting our newly minted plan, we determine and assign next actions. This gets the show on the road.

User assistance

Some points on documenting and presenting your plan:

1. Documenting the plan: (a) Your organization may already have standards for such things; or (b) my last book [1] had some suggestions that were simple and got all the stuff in

there; or (c) if you want to be more formal, you could use the recommendations in something like BS 6079 [5].

2. In presenting the plan, a presentation format that we find works especially well is the following:

- Background to the project, in particular the "baggage";

- The options identified and the one being recommended;

- For that option—a management summary ("the big picture"):

  · What's being delivered;

  · The delivery date and schedule;

  · The effort and budget;

  · Quality measures;

  · Who the project manager is;

  · The principal assumptions upon which the plan is based;

  · Any issues that remain outstanding.

- The plan:

  · High-level (fit on a page or a slide) Gantt chart. (While we may not want to see the lower level detail, we reserve the right to ask questions about it.)

- Evidence that the plan contains contingency;

- A PSI calculation.

How to run projects using the least amount of work possible and still have a successful outcome.

3 Running Projects (Steps 6–10)

Questions

? Q.1 You are a consultant running a project for a client. Jobs that are in the project plan and that have to be done by the client's people are continuously late or done badly. Whose responsibility is this?

(a) Yours personally.

(b) Your company's.

(c) The client's people's.

(d) The client's management.

? Q.2 You are the project manager of a technical project, and you also have technical jobs to do on the project. The result is that you're insanely busy with never enough time for everything. If you can only pick one thing to do, do you choose:

(a) The technical jobs—on the basis that if these are not done, the project won't get done.

(b) Ask for an "admin. person" to "update the plan" while you concentrate on the technical work.

(c) The project management jobs.

(d) None of the above.

? Q.3 Part of your project has been subcontracted to another organization. The separation is very clear, and the interface between the two pieces of the project is carefully defined. You're paying them a fat fee for the project management of their bit. You have no visibility of the progress of the subcontracted part, and you're starting to get a feeling that all is not well. What do you do?

(a) Get some evidence to support your hunch; then, wade in there and sort it out.

(b) Take the view that you're paying for project management— it's their problem.

(c) As in (b) but take the additional precaution of writing a "cover-your-ass" memo pointing this out to everybody.

(d) Take no action until the excrement hits the ventilating device and then do (a).

Answers

Q.1
(a) 5 points: Right.
(b) 5 points: Right again.
(c) 2 points: I suppose it depends on how you interpret the word "responsible." For me, it means your butt is on the line for it.
(d) 2 points: Ditto.

Q.2
(a) 0 points: Yes, they have to get done, but this is not the right answer to the question.
(b) 0 points: In my opinion, you're on very dangerous ground here. If the admin. person is merely providing secretarial assistance, then you haven't solved the problem. If he or she is actually "working" the plan, then he or she has become the project manager! I have never seen this solution solve this problem.
(c) 5 points: Yes. Sure, your technical jobs need to get done, but if you neglect the project management, then it's likely that all the other technical work—perhaps, barring yours—will go to hell.
(d) 0 points: The right answer is (c).

Q.3
(a) 5 points: On the money. Sadly (for you!), it's still your responsibility.
(b) 1 point: But only because I'm feeling generous.
(c) 2 points: But if your business is successful projects, then this isn't going far enough.
(d) 2 points: Better late than never, but (a) is a better answer.

Scores

15 points: Good. You're my kind of project manager.

12 points: I'd hire you, but I'd rather have a 15 working for me.

Less than 12: No thanks. No need to send in your resume at this stage.

Introduction

"Plan the work and work the plan" is the old adage. In Chapter 2 we focused our attention on the "plan the work" part of it. Here we describe the tools to "work the plan."

Once the project has been planned, then—theoretically, at least—keeping it on target is very simple. If you could bite off what the plan says each week or each month and somehow make those things happen, then the project would remain on target for that week or month. If you could do this repeatedly, then the project would always remain on target. This is what structured project management sets out to do.

The framework for doing all of this is the project manager's weekly routine, which consists of the following constituents:

- The Monday meetings;

- The project manager's daily routine;

- Status reporting.

These are fitted onto the week as follows:

- Monday: Monday meetings plus daily routine;

- Tuesday: Daily routine;

- Wednesday: Daily routine;

- Thursday: Daily routine;

- Friday: Daily routine plus status report.

These are described in turn.

Monday meetings

The Monday meetings are the first part of making sure we do what the plan says in a particular week. They determine how much of the project needs to be "bitten off" that week.

Monday meetings take place as close to the beginning of the week as possible—hence the name! Monday is the best. If it has been, for example, a holiday weekend so that the week starts on Tuesday, then the Monday meetings take place on Tuesday! It is vital that the Monday meetings are held religiously every week; they need to become a part of the culture of the organization. They are vital because they give the organization a weekly chance to re-synchronize all of their projects.

Former British Prime Minister Harold Wilson is credited with having said that "A week is a long time in politics." A week is also a long time in a project. In addition, given that there are fewer than 50 weeks in the year (once holidays are taken into account), weeks represent a significant unit of project currency, which we would do well not to fritter away.

The Monday meetings quite simply determine exactly what needs to be achieved by close of business that Friday. This is done by looking at the plans for the particular projects. Monday meetings can be held with just the project managers, or team members can be involved when necessary.

Involving just the project managers has the advantage that it leaves the troops free to do the work of the project. The disadvantage is that, especially if the project manager is not fully up to speed *au fait* with the state of the project, wrong decisions will be made—mistakes that the team members might have caught. The choice is dependent on a number of issues, notably the quality of the following:

- The people working for you;

- The project management of the project.

If in doubt, involve the members. They can always leave if they find it's wasting their time.

Daily routine

The daily routine implements the concept that the plan/model that we have built is the instrumentation with which we can drive our project. The plan tells us what should be happening on the project. By comparing this with what is actually happening, we can determine the following:

- Corrective actions that need to be taken;

- The true status of the project.

Clearly we can only do this if we have a plan/model of the kind we have described in the first place.

During the course of the daily routine, a person would do the following:

- Look down the line representing today on your plan and examine all of the jobs clustered within a week either side of this line. These are the activities that should currently be going on. Now compare these with the situation on the ground and make changes to the plan accordingly.

- Now do the same with things that lie in the future. (Think of this as the items that lie "to the right" of the line that represents today.) When the project began you may have had to make assumptions because you did not have any knowledge about these things. Now, as a result of where you are in the project, you may have better or even complete knowledge of these issues. Substitute the knowledge for assumptions wherever you can. Then update the plan accordingly.

As a result of having done these two things—we call them "the current stuff" and "the future stuff"—a number of things may have happened to your plan. We use military parlance and call them code green, code yellow, code orange, and code red.

Code green

The project remains on target—that is, there has been absolutely no change in the following:

- What is to be delivered;
- When it is to be delivered;
- The total effort involved/the project budget;
- Any quality parameters.

Similarly, no change is likely to cause concern in either of the following:

- Individual elapsed time for jobs;
- Individual job efforts or budgets.

Code yellow

There has been slippage in one or more of the above parameters, but it can be fixed by drawing from the plan's contingency.

Code orange

There has been slippage in one or more of the above parameters, and it can't be fixed by drawing on the contingency because all of the contingency has been used up.

Code red

There has been slippage in one or more of the above parameters, and we're actually into negative contingency (i.e., we're now trying to fix the slippage using functionality, people, effort, and financial and quality resources that we don't actually have).

Apart from slippage in the plan, the other factor that materially affects the outcome here is whether or not assumptions upon which the plan was originally based have been breached (i.e., whether or not there has been a change requiring change control).

If there has, then that is quite a different matter than if there hasn't. You can't be expected to build a plan that holds in all circumstances. That is one of the principal reasons you have assumptions in the first place. It is also the reason why many projects go wrong, because project managers believe precisely this—that their plan must hold in all circumstances. Anyone with half a brain can see that this isn't true!

Table 3.1 explains the options open to the project manager depending on whether he or she hits a code green, yellow, orange, or red and whether or not change control is being implemented.

Status reporting

Most status reports aren't worth the virgin pulp that went into the paper they're written on. The reason for this is that, by and large, they follow the style that we in ETP call "a day at the beach." This refers to those essays we all (I suspect) wrote when we were at school entitled "A Day at the Beach." Full of color, excitement, characters, incident, a certain pathos, and a compulsory happy ending, they tell us absolutely nothing about the state of the project, other than that everyone is very busy and having a good time and is hopeful—I use the word very deliberately—about the outcome.

If you want a different analogy, try this one, which originated at a workshop I gave a couple of years ago to a telecommunications company. In structured project management, we say that you need to filter the information coming out of the project so that sensible analyses can be passed on to your customer, your management, and your team. I used to describe this as acting like a low-pass filter, which—insofar as I understand it—removes a lot of the extremes (both good—above the line —and bad—below the line) so that an averaged signal gets through (i.e., it does what is shown in Figure 3.1).

I mentioned this in the workshop, and they asked whether I had heard of a rectifier. A rectifier, they explained, removed part of the signal (i.e., it did what Figure 3.2 does—it removes the bad news).

However, they topped this by then telling me about the bridge rectifier. The bridge rectifier is shown in Figure 3.3.

Table 3.1 Daily Routine Action Diagram

Code?	Monitoring Step 7 Analysis Change Control		Control Step 7 Action		Reporting Step 8 Action Change Control		A Succession of This Color?
	Yes	No	Yes	No	Yes	No	
Green— no change to plan	A change has occurred	Your model (i.e., pre-diction) is correct and there has been no change to the plan since you last ran the daily routine	Implement change con-trol using steps 1–5(a)	No further action required	Report that change control has been implemented	No further action required	If Change Control = No, then this is no problem. This is actu-ally what you want to happen on your project. If Change Control = Yes, then this is good. It means that every time a change occurs, you're (a) capturing it and (b) dealing with it correctly.
Yellow— slip but fixable by using contingency	A change has occurred	Note that some contingency has been used up	Implement change con-trol using steps 1–5(a)	No further action required	Report that change control has been implemented	Low level warning; report that some contingency has been used up. This could cause the schedule to "come under pressure" depending on how much contingency is gone.	If Change Control = No, then repeated code yellows mean that you are continuously draw-ing on your contin-gency. This represents a deterioration on the project. If Change Control = Yes, then this is good. It means that every time a change occurs, you're (a) capturing it and (b) dealing with it correctly.

Table 3.1 (continued)

Code?	Monitoring Step 7 Analysis Change Control		Control Step 7 Action		Reporting Step 8 Action Change Control		A Succession of This Color?
	Yes	No	Yes	No	Yes	No	
Orange— slip, not fixable because all contingency used up (i.e., reached limit of contingency)	A change has occurred	Note that all the contingency is gone	Implement change control using steps 1–5(a)	Wait for a preset period of time to see if there is any improvement. If not you've got a Code Red on your hands.	Report that change has been implemented	High-level warning that with all contingency gone, unless there is some improvement we will be forced to slip the project and renegotiate deadlines, resources, budgets, etc.	If Change Control = No, then repeated code oranges mean that you are running continuously at the limit of your contingency. This is a lethal situation to be in. If Change Control = Yes, Then this is good. It means that every time a change occurs, you're (a) capturing it and (b) dealing with it correctly.
Red— slip, not fixable and contingency blown (i.e., gone beyond limit of contingency)	A change has occurred	In negative contingency	Implement change control using steps 1–5(a)	Renegotiate the project	Report that change control has been implemented	COME CLEAN— tell the powers that be that there's a problem	You only need one

Figure 3.1
Low-pass filter.

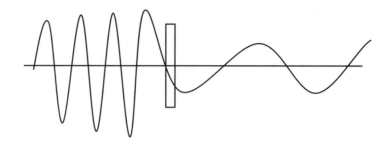

Figure 3.2   Rectifier.

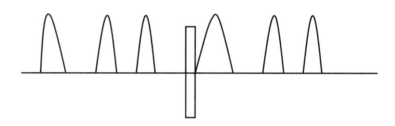

Figure 3.3
Bridge rectifier.

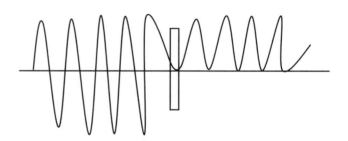

The bridge rectifier turns bad news into good news. In my opinion, most status reports that you come across are bridge-rectified. In project management, this is equivalent to removing the bad news.

In structured project management we suggest that status reports are done every Friday. Thus, the Monday meetings and the Friday status reports "bracket" the week. The Monday meetings determine what needs to be done; the status reports say what actually got done.

Sensible status reports need to be structured such that they do the following:

- Give a high-level description of the state of the project;

- Justify this with a next layer of detail centered on structured project management's four parameters—functionality, elapsed time, effort (cost), and quality;

- Point to where the remainder of the detail about the project can be found.

This is not hard to do. In terms of the high-level description, I've seen a number of different ways it can work:

1. Check the box: "The project is on target. Yes/No. Please check one."

2. Red/amber/green: This is an approach that I am very fond of and that we cover in more detail in Part Two of the book.

3. Key questions: The report could begin with the answers to a set of key questions, such as the following:

- Will any of the project milestones be missed?

- Are there any problems with estimates?

- Are there any functional or technical problems?

- Are there any quality issues?

- Are there any people problems?

- Are there any opportunities for improvement?

For the next layer of detail, the most important thing, in my opinion, is to provide a context to that status report. What I mean by this is that it's no good, for example, giving a delivery date, if we don't understand the significance of that date in the broader scheme of things. Giving a single date is much less useful than giving the change history of the delivery date:

- Here's what the date was originally.

- Here's what it is now.

- Here's its change history.

Clearly you can also do this for things like effort, budget, and the quality measure.

A final point has to do with the way some day-at-the-beach status reports also have a certain therapeutic value to the project manager. I'm referring to the way in which some project managers use the status reports to complain about their lot. For example: "The users are not committing the resources they originally promised to the project," or "There is a lack of management commitment to this project," or "The quality of the stuff being received from the subcontractor is woeful," or "A project manager's lot is not a happy one." (I'm kidding—about the last one, at any rate.) While whining like this may get certain things off the project manager's chest, it doesn't necessarily advance the cause of the project.

Far better, instead of the regular whining, is to say the following:

- Here's the issue.

- Here's what I want done about it.

- Here's when I want it done by.

- If it ain't fixed, here's what's going to happen.

The medicinal value may be lower, but it's more likely to achieve the desired result.

This chapter's User Assistance section contains a complete example of a status report for a software development project. (The names have been changed to protect the innocent, so it's possible that the report may not make a great deal of sense. It is the format and nature of the content that's important rather than the content itself.)

User assistance

Status report

Project: Great Product Version 1.2.
Report: 14
Date: 21 October 1998
Project Manager: Frank
Team: Rachel, Debbie
Declan, Steve
Mary
Distribution: As above plus Bernadette, Hugh, Dan, Pedroetra, Tedim, File + Tell anyone else who's interested.
Overall status:

First week of system testing (version 1.1.0), testing both on Windows 95 and 97. 56 bugs reported. A new release (1.1.1) will be available this Friday, 24 October.

Current dates are the following:

- Beta availability: November 17, 1998;
- General availability: January 19, 1999.

Detailed status
Project scope

The scope of this project is defined in the Project Plan and associated Requirements Spec. version 0.8. Table 3.2 provides information on the delivery date change history; Table 3.3 provides information on the change history of the estimated costs to complete; and Table 3.4 compares the planned and actual budgets.

Quality

We are using mean time to defect (MTTD) as a measure of quality. We are proposing to ship with an MTTD of 45 hours. Table 3.5 presents quality information.

Table 3.2   Delivery Date Change History

Date of Change	Reason for Change	Into Beta Date	General Availability Date
	Original dates	1 May 1998	1 Sept. 1998
9 May 1998	See section 1 of the project plan	24 Nov. 1998	23 Jan. 1999
27 May 1998	Added an extra person for a couple of weeks	12 Nov. 1998	12 Jan. 1999
2 July 1998	Some improvements due to use of Mary	3 Nov. 1998	5 Jan. 1999
14 Oct. 1998	Slip in development schedule	17 Nov. 1998	19 Jan. 1999

Table 3.3   Estimated Cost to Complete — Change History

Date of Change	Reason for Change	Estimated Cost to Complete (in £)
9 May 1998	As described in plan	£49,000
20 May 1998	Slight overestimation in costs of software licenses required	£48,500
27 May 1998	Addition of extra software engineer for two weeks	£51,000
11 Aug. 1998	Overestimate of legal fees and cost of manufacturing	£44,000
29 Sept. 1998	Slight underestimate of size and error handling required	£44,500

Table 3.4   Planned and Actual Budgets

Item	Original Budget	Current Budget	Spent to Date
Technical consultancy	£3,000	£6,000	£6,000
Software licenses	£2,000	£1,500	£1,200
Technical writing	£8,000	£8,000	£0
Trademark/patent/legal	£10,000	£8,000	£820
Final package design	£6,000	£6,000	£0
Manufacture	£20,000	£15,000	£0
Totals	£49,000	£44,500	£8,020

Table 3.5   Quality Information

Week	Total Testing Time	Number of Bugs Found	MTTD
13 October 1998	2½ hours (Frank) + 2 hours (Steve)	56	5 minutes

Planned for next week

Debbie and Rachel will work on bug fixing; Steve will offer design consultancy; and Frank will do testing.

Other issues

The next status meeting takes place on Monday, 27 October. On the agenda are the following:

1. Things achieved during last period based on timesheets and status on plan;

2. Bug reports;

3. Change control requests;

4. Planning of next period's work using timesheets;

5. Setting next meeting date.

You're handed a large tome and told that this is the project plan, or you're at a presentation of such a plan. There are masses and masses of Powerpoint, Gantt charts, PERT, critical path—the whole shooting gallery. This chapter will tell you how to quickly determine whether what they're giving you is any good.

4 Assessing Project Plans (Steps 1–5)

Questions

? Q.1 You are running a project, and you finally come to the conclusion that J. Smith, who works for you, definitely isn't up to the piece of the project he or she has been given. You've decided to remove him or her from the project. Assuming you carry through this decision, what's going to be your *immediate* priority?

    (a) The impact on J. Smith's state of mind, aspirations, career, morale, etc.

    (b) How you stand legally having removed him or her.

    (c) Whether your boss will back you in your action.

    (d) Finding somebody else to do J. Smith's jobs.

? Q.2 You have a superstar working on your project. He or she is highly skilled, experienced, and motivated—and doing what he or she loves to do. What is most likely to make such superstars unhappy?

    (a) You micromanaging them.

(b) Being given uninteresting work.

(c) You questioning their judgment and decisions.

(d) Low or infrequent salary hikes.

? Q.3 Most of the people who work on projects are neither the duds described in question 1 nor the geniuses of question 2. To keep these people motivated, which of the following would be best?

(a) Social events—barbecues, parties, and so on.

(b) Involving them in the planning.

(c) Ensuring that, via status reporting and other communication, they stay informed about the big picture, their part in it, and progress on the project.

(d) Freebies—T-shirts, mugs, that sort of thing, to foster a team spirit.

Answers

Q.1
(a) 0 points: Call me callous if you like, but no, this is not the first thing you have to get sorted.
(b) 1 point: I'd like to think you checked this before you did what you did.
(c) 1 point: Similarly for this. Also the strongest answer you can have for your boss (and the legal eagles, by the way) is to have the evidence upon which you based your decision.
(d) 5 points: If enough of the jobs don't get done, the project doesn't succeed.

Q.2
(a) 5 points: Yes, nothing surer. A waste of your time and quite counterproductive.
(b) 5 points: Yes again.
(c) 5 points: And again.
(d) 3 points: To some extent, but not as much as you'd think.

Q.3
(a) 1 point: Bread and circuses! I don't think so.
(b) 5 points: Yep.
(c) 5 points: And again.
(d) 1/2 points: C'mon. Be serious.

Scores

15 points: Easy to get a high score here.

10–14 points: B minus. Could do better.

Less than 10: Were you reading the book or watching television?

Introduction

Now that the first three chapters are behind us, many of the chapters in the remainder of this part of the book can be mercifully brief. This one is no exception.

In assessing a plan, you are basically looking for evidence that the author has satisfied the requirements of steps 1–5. If you use these as your checklist or benchmark, then you will be able to home in on the key issues of the plan very quickly. A useful by-product of this is that you will gain a reputation for being somebody who can spot flaws in a plan a mile off.

A situation where this is particularly useful is in dealing with subcontractors. (Remember question 3 at the beginning of Chapter 3.) Make them present their plan and subject it to steps 1–5 for scrutiny. (You'll have some entertaining moments—I guarantee it.) If the plan doesn't pass, either send them packing, send them back to the drawing board, or ask for a reduction in the project management part of their proposal on the basis that you're doing a lot of it for them.

Here we give you a quick checklist for assessing a plan. The checklist is organized into three levels, and you go through them in turn. The real turkeys don't make it past level 1. That way you don't waste your time. The checklist has been filled out for a hypothetical project. A blank checklist is also provided.

User assistance

Title: Review of PENGUIN project plan

Overview: This document was written after a day-long formal review of the PENGUIN project plan from Acme Software. The review followed the standard ETP process. The level 1 checks were performed first, and the plan passed these. As the level 1 checks had sufficient yes's to pass, the level 2 checks were then performed. The level 3 checks were not needed. A detailed risk analysis was then performed with the assistance of the project manager. This identified many high-probability risks, which are documented with appropriate contingency plans.

Author:

Date:

Review Summary

Customer:	Acme Software	Project:	PENGUIN
P.M.:			

Items delivered:

Phase 1 project plan, Server}

Phase 1 project plan, Client } 1 document

Phase 2 project plan

2 docs.

Introduction:

This plan review is based on the documents received and on discussions with the project manager.

This is a review of a project plan. It is not a review of a project manager or project team. Please do not take offense at any of the comments made. The purpose of this review is to identify areas of concern in the planning process that could cause problems during the project. The comments are intended to be positive and constructive and to assist the project manager and team in achieving the project goals.

Overall comments:

This is a clearly defined, well-structured project plan. It has a PSI score of 60 at this stage, which is positive.

The goal of the project is quite clear, and the functionality required is clearly specified. Because the new product is based on an existing product, the effort estimates are likely to be more accurate than usual.

The areas of concern are the standard ones of a very tight time scale and potential for overallocation and nonavailability of resources. All development resources are allocated for five days per week until November, and testing resources are not yet defined. The perfect availability of all resources is critical to the maintenance of the schedule. These are all serious concerns.

Given the above concerns, we have identified 12 areas of risk to the successful completion of the project and have proposed a contingency plan to alleviate the potential danger of each of these.

Checklist for Carrying Out the Level 1 Checks

Are the contents of the plan clear and sufficient? Is there:	Y/N
A clear understanding of goal (e.g., reference to work spec, deliverables identified, dates in plan)?	Y
A structured list of tasks?	Y
A Gantt chart?	Y
Key milestones? Start, end of development, QA, deliverables?	Y
Resources assigned to tasks?	Y
Resource loadings supplied?	Y
Risk analysis/contingency highlighted?	Y
Comments: A well-structured plan with a lot of detail. It is cleanly divided into client and server tasks.	

Is the task list in sufficient detail and complete?	Y/N
Sufficient major, high-level tasks identified?	Y
Is the product broken down into its components?	Y
Are the tasks in sufficient detail to control (would expect 5 days)?	Y
Are sufficient detailed tasks identified?	Y
Are task dependencies identified?	Y
Does the WBS match the work spec?	Y
Comments: Over 250 tasks, but a few of these are too long to be accurately controlled.	

Is a Gantt chart supplied?	Y/N
(This is automatically true if an MS project plan is given.) If not, is it easy to get a graphical overview of the project?	Y
Comments: This is a well-structured, fully defined Gantt chart. All dates are driven from the project start date, which is important for ease of maintenance.	

Is it possible to see the key milestones?	Y/N
Are the start milestones very visible?	Y
Are there enough of them?	N
Are they linked to the rest of the tasks?	Y
Are the end milestones very visible	Y
Are there enough of them?	N
Are they linked to the rest of the tasks?	Y

Comments: There are not sufficient milestones identified in the plan. However, the plan is very well structured so this is not a serious issue.

Are resource names available against each task?	Y/N
Are individual people names on most immediate tasks?	Y
Have all tasks got resources assigned (either named or generic)?	Y

Comments: This is complete.

Is the resource loading appropriate?	Y/N
(This is easy if MS project is used.)	
Are all resources underutilized?	N
Have public holidays been catered for?	Y
Have resource holidays been catered for?	Y
Are resources scheduled < 40 hours per week?	Y

Comments: Most resources are scheduled for five days per week for the duration of the development. Each resource is therefore a potential source of time scale slippage. The number of testers required has not yet been identified.

What is the PSI score for the planning part of the project?	Y/N
(Must be high, at least 50–60, since the goal is already well-defined.)	
Is goal >15 (20)	Y
Is list of jobs >15 (18)	Y
Is one leader >6 (7)	Y
Are resources assigned >7 (8)	Y
Is contingency > 7 (7)	Y

Comments: Total PSI of 60, which is very positive at this stage. The contingency score assumes that the contingency plans are accepted. The major risk is the extremely tight time scale.

Checklist for Carrying Out the Level 2 Checks

Analyze schedule duration
Analyze effort distribution

Phase	Schedule	%	Effort	%
Total	170 days		880 days	
Requirements analysis				
High-level design				
Low-level design				
Development				
System testing				
Documentation				
Implementation/packaging				

Comments: A detailed formal analysis of the schedule and effort has not yet been undertaken. No effort figures are available for the testing.

The effort of 880 days above is actually required in 170 elapsed days. This implies an average of just over 5 resources per day during the development phase.

Review each task on the critical path

How many tasks in total?	~250
How many tasks on the critical path?	~ 40
Is effort on each okay?	Y
Is information supplied to allow effort to be assessed?	Y
Is schedule for each okay?	Y
Is information supplied to allow schedule to be assessed?	N
Is named resource assigned?	Y
Resource is not overloaded?	Y
Reasonable assumptions documented about resource availability?	N

Comments: The critical path is in the client and the testing area.

Major risks

The current schedule shows the finish date as March 31, 1998. This is the most optimistic possible date and is therefore not realistic. There is little contingency for anything to go wrong.

We have identified a number of major risk areas and have determined contingency plans to address these risks. These contingency plans must be adhered to if the project is to be completed by the required date.

1. **Risk:** All of the resources defined are required to be available throughout the project.

    Contingency:

    Client team: We will hire an additional VB programmer for the client team. This programmer needs to be hired immediately. A contractor might be suitable for this position. This will provide contingency for the possibility of losing a resource on the client team due to illness or leaving. However, there are key people whose absence would definitely move the end date. There is no appropriate contingency identified for this.

    Server team: Fred or Charlie will act as contingency for unavailability of server team members. This would obviously adversely impact other projects. A decision needs to be made as to the relative priority of PENGUIN and other projects in this eventuality. An alternative is to hire an additional programmer for servers, but as there is currently a shortage of available skills on the market, it is unlikely that this will be possible.

2. **Risk:** There is very little contingency in the client estimates. If any of the tasks are underestimated or if there any surprises, then this will most likely affect the delivery date.

    Contingency: The client progress will be reviewed at the end of August. At this time it will be decided whether or not a contractor VB programmer is required. An additional contingency may be to move the proposed language independence enhancements to phase 2. (This requires technical investigation as to feasibility and benefits.)

3. **Risk:** There is no technical design authority for the server team. This could impact the delivery date.

    Contingency: Fred and Charlie must each be available ½ day per week throughout the PENGUIN cycle. In addition, 10 days of each have been allocated for technical assistance. In the event that this time is not sufficient, then further requests for their time will be made. Again, a decision needs to be made as to the relative priority of PENGUIN and other projects in this eventuality.

4. **Risk:** The project manager of all existing PENGUIN releases is moving to other projects. Losing his or her product knowledge and detailed PENGUIN technical background may have an unforeseen impact on delivery date.

    Contingency: He or she must be available one day per week as a consultant on the PENGUIN project.

5. **Risk:** There is no time allocated for interaction between customers and the development team. This may not be realistic.

    Contingency: George will act as the sole interface between customers and the development team. If this is not possible, or if detailed technical consultancy is required, then Reggie must be available as an interface.

6. **Risk:** At this stage of the development cycle there appears to be a lack of enthusiasm or motivation in the development team.

    Contingency: We must start the implementation phase immediately and keep developers busy writing code. Any unnecessary process, procedure, or interruption must be eliminated.

7. **Risk:** ALBATROSS support requirements may deflect resources from PENGUIN development.

    Contingency: There is ½ a person day per week allocated from both the client and the server teams to assist the support department. This allocation will be closely monitored. Any excesses to this will cause a delay to the project.

8. **Risk:** The high-level designs have not been signed off by product management or by QA. Any significant changes to these can potentially affect the delivery date.

    Contingency: There is no contingency provided for significant changes to the current designs.

9. **Risk:** The QA cycle has been defined to be three months duration. Detailed estimates for QA will not be available until down the line, so the QA team cannot guarantee that this estimate is accurate.

    Contingency: The plan will be updated to reflect any changes in the QA cycle estimate. If QA estimate is greater than three months, then additional people must be hired for QA.

The assumptions that have been made include the following:

1. All of the resources specified are available throughout the project.

2. Client estimates are correct.

3. Fred and Charlie are available ½ a day per week each throughout the project.

4. Fred and Charlie are available for a further 10 days each (at short notice) sometime between August and the product release.

5. There will be no interaction between the development team and customers.

6. There will be a maximum of ½ a person day per week allocated to assist support.

7. The high-level designs will not require significant changes as a result of review by product management and QA.

8. No additional requirements will be included in PENGUIN release.

Following is a blank checklist:

Title:

Overview:

Author:

Date:

Review Summary

Customer:	Project:
P.M.:	

Items delivered:

Introduction:

Overall comments:

Checklist for Carrying Out the Level 1 Checks

Are the contents of the plan clear and sufficient? Is there:	Y/N
A clear understanding of goal (e.g., reference to work spec, deliverables identified, dates in plan)?	
A structured list of tasks?	
A Gantt chart?	
Key milestones?	
Start, end of development, QA, deliverables?	
Resources assigned to tasks?	
Resource loadings supplied?	
Risk analysis/contingency highlighted?	
Comments:	

Is the task list in sufficient detail and complete?	Y/N
Sufficient major, high-level tasks identified?	
Is the product broken down into its components?	
Are the tasks in sufficient detail to control (would expect 5 days)?	
Are sufficient detailed tasks identified?	
Are task dependencies identified?	
Does the WBS match the work spec?	
Comments:	

Is a Gantt chart supplied?	Y/N
(This is automatically true if an MS project plan is given.)	
If not, is it easy to get a graphical overview of the project?	
Comments:	

Is it possible to see the key milestones?	Y/N
Are the start milestones very visible? Are there enough of them? Are they linked to the rest of the tasks? Are the end milestones very visible? Are there enough of them? Are they linked to the rest of the tasks?	
Comments:	

Are resource names available against each task?	Y/N
Are individual people names on most immediate tasks? Have all tasks got resources assigned (either named or generic)?	
Comments:	

Is the resource loading appropriate?	Y/N
(This is easy if MS project is used.) Are all resources underutilized? Have public holidays been catered for? Have resource holidays been catered for? Are resources scheduled < 40 hours per week?	
Comments:	

What is the PSI score for the planning part of the project?	Y/N
(Must be high, at least 50–60, since the goal is already well-defined.) Is goal > 15 nn Is list of jobs > 15 nn Is one leader > 6 nn Are resources assigned > 7 nn Is contingency > 7 nn	
Comments:	

Checklist for Carrying Out the Level 2 Checks

Analyze schedule duration

Analyze effort distribution

Phase	Schedule	%	Effort	%
Total				
Requirements analysis				
High-level design				
Low-level design				
Development				
System testing				
Documentation				
Implementation/packaging				
Comments:				

Review each task on the critical path

How many tasks in total?	
How many tasks on the critical path?	
Is effort on each okay?	
Is information supplied to allow effort to be assessed?	
Is schedule for each okay?	
Is information supplied to allow schedule to be assessed?	
Is named resource assigned?	
Resource is not overloaded?	
Reasonable assumptions documented about resource availability?	
Comments:	

Major risks

We have identified a number of major risk areas and have determined contingency plans to address these risks. These contingency plans must be adhered to if the project is to be completed by the required date.

1.   **Risk:**

     Contingency:

The following assumptions have been made:

1.

2.

3.

4.

5.

6.

7.

8.

9.

10.

Assessing plans is one thing. Assessing projects is a bit more tricky. The project is under way; people have been assigned; money, time, and resources are being consumed. Here's what to do in this situation.

5 Assessing Projects (Steps 1–10)

Questions

? Q.1 You've inherited a project and, having assessed it using steps 1–5, notice that in doing this, you weren't automatically accepting the previous project manager's "baggage"—you've discovered that it looks like it will be ending three months *ahead* of the previously published schedule. What do you do next?

(a) Tell the team.

(b) Say nothing.

(c) Tell all the stakeholders.

(d) None of the above.

? Q.2 You work in an organization where, if they see contingency in a plan, they take it out. (No, I'm sure you couldn't imagine such a place!) Putting hidden contingency into your plan is a morally justifiable thing to do.

(a) Yes.

(b) No.

(c) Not sure.

(d) I'd put it in explicitly and defend it to the death.

? Q.3 Assuming you have no estimating data from completed projects to go by, when putting contingency into your plan, which of these would be the best approach?

(a) Two percent.

(b) Ten percent.

(c) Fifteen percent.

(d) As much as you can possibly get away with.

Answers

Q.1

(a) 0 points: In doing this you quite neatly give away a potential three month's contingency.

(b) 5 points: Yes, for the present. Nobody is saying to keep silent and one day jump out of a cake yelling "surprise!" That wouldn't win you any friends, and, even if it did, you'd have huge credibility problems next time out. What we are recommending is to give away this three month's contingency piecemeal so that the project turns out exactly like you said it would. Remember that, in a sense, your estimate is no more or less valid than that of the previous project manager. Your plan is a prediction just like his or hers. In other words, the three months may be just a figment of your imagination.

(c) 0 points: And I'd give you a minus score if I could. Same as (a) except much worse. Completely unforgivable.

(d) 2 points: Provided you accept the essential point in answer (b), then there are other ways to skin this particular cat.

Q.2

(a) 5 points: We could argue about it, but I personally believe that it is. Someday they'll thank you for it.

(b) 4 points: I'll give you four for being so upright, but maybe you should consider finding a less stressful organization. Happily, they're becoming more commonplace.

(c) 4 points: I'm sure—but a moral theologian might have a field day here. Four because I respect your point of view.

(d) 5 points: Best answer. Someday they'll have to wake up and smell the coffee. You may as well be the one to do the waking. On the other hand, life is short. Maybe there are other things you want to do with yours.

Q.3
(a) 1 point: Better then nothing, but it won't get you very far.
(b) 2 points: Better.
(c) 3 points: Better still.
(d) 5 points: Works for me. There aren't too many ways to improve your estimating, and by far the best one is to record data from previous projects (successful or not). If you don't do this, then when you come to estimate a new project, you are essentially guessing. You've just given it a more respectable name. In that case, you'd better have as much contingency as you can find. You're going to need it.

Scores

15 points: Top marks here is tough enough. Good work.

14 points: Yeah, those moral dilemmas are tricky.

Less than 14: Contingency can save your bacon, not to mention your career. If I were you, I'd reconsider my attitude toward it.

Introduction

Some years ago, I was bidding for a piece of business with a large insurance company. The company had a project that had gone off the rails, and it was looking for somebody to rescue it. By rescuing it, they meant figuring out where the project had gone wrong and putting a plan in place to get it back on the rails.

Using the 10 steps as your benchmark, it is possible to figure out what went wrong comfortably in two days, almost irrespective of the size of the project. During the two days you generally do the following:

- Talk with the project manager (and maybe some or all of the team): ½ day;

- Document what you found out: ½ day;

- Meet with the same or some additional people to do some more detective work: ½ day;

- Update documentation: ½ day.

Throwing in a bit for contingency and profit, I did a little proposal for five person-days plus travel expenses.

My bid was turned down, and I discovered afterward that the work went instead to a big six (as they were then) consultancy firm that had bid six person-weeks for the "figure out what went wrong" part and at a much higher daily rate than I had.

The moral of this story? Well, depending on your point of view, there were numerous lessons to be learned. From the point of view of this book, we want to show you how to assess projects quickly and effectively.

The User Assistance section shows a questionnaire we use for doing this.

User assistance

Project Assessment Summary Form

Project:

Project manager:

Project sponsor:

Project documents reviewed:

Date:

Summary of results
Project planning probability of success indicator (PSI): /70
Assessment Color
Red = In trouble
Blue = No plan exists
Amber = Some problems
Green = On target

Areas of concern

Recommendations

Introduction

This project plan review is based on only the documents and interview data collected. This is a review of the project plan. It is not a review of the project manager or his or her performance.

Purpose

The purpose of this review is to identify areas of concern in the project that could cause problems during the project or put the final deliverable at risk. The comments are intended to be positive and constructive and to assist the project manager in achieving the project goals.

Project goal

Tasks

All tasks have/(do not have) names resources assigned, so it is/(is not) clear which resources are required at what points in time.

Because these resources are/(are not) named it is/(is not) assumed that these resources will/(will not) be available when required.

Project leadership/project organization

Project resourcing

Contingency margins for error, managing expectations

There is an/(is no) indication of contingency plans, and this area is/(is not) of concern. All/(Some) resources are heavily loaded, and there is/(is no) indication of what will happen if staff become indisposed/unavailable or if estimates do not work out in practice.

Project Auditor _____   Date: _____
               [   ]

Structured Project Management Audit

Part 1: project planning   Max probability of success indication
(PSI): 70%

Project name and number: _____

Project sponsor: _____

Project manager: _____

Step 1: Visualize the Goal (Max PSI: 20)

1. Definition of the project goal or final deliverable (PSI: 6)

Does the goal statement comprehensively describe what is to
be done in terms of:

Functionality	Y/N
Effort (cost)?	Y/N
Time?	Y/N
Quality?	Y/N

Is the goal statement:

Simple?	Y/N
Measurable?	Y/N
Achievable?	Y/N
Realistic?	Y/N
Timely?	Y/N

PSI:

2. Deliverables, subgoals (PSI: 4)

Are all deliverables, which will result from the project listed?
Y/N

Are all significant consequences (business benefits or impacts
such as reduced costs, additional revenues, enhanced
customer service) that will result from the project listed?   Y/N

PSI:

3. Project completion criteria (PSI: 2)

Is there an indicator of when we know that the project is
over?   Y/N

PSI:

4. Project deliverables quality acceptance criteria (PSI: 2)

Is there an indicator to the customer/client that the project is over? Y/N

PSI:

5. Assumptions/dependencies/critical success factors (PSI: 3)

Are all the assumptions on which the project is based listed? Y/N

Have all the dependencies with other projects been identified and listed? Y/N

Have all critical success factors affecting the project been identified and listed? Y/N

PSI:

6. Project stakeholders (PSI: 3)

Have all stakeholders with an interest in the project been identified and listed? Y/N

Have all their needs been captured in the project goal statement? Y/N

Have all requirements consequent from their needs been included in the goal statement? Y/N

Have they reviewed and approved the project scope and goal(s)? Y/N

PSI:

Step 2: Make a List of Jobs to Be Done (Max PSI: 20)

7. Work breakdown structure (WBS) (PSI: 10)

Does a list of *all* the tasks to be done to complete the project exist? Y/N

Does the WBS contain an estimate of the effort (work) that each task requires? Y/N

Does the WBS list all assumptions made? Y/N

Does the WBS contain project management effort of 8–12% of the total project effort? Y/N

PSI:

8. Gantt (or other) chart (PSI: 6)

Does a visual chart or representation showing work tasks phased over time exist?   Y/N

Does it show the main phases of the project?   Y/N

Does it show the length of these phases and how they relate to each other?   Y/N

Does it show the amount of work (effort) in each phase?   Y/N

PSI:

9. Milestones (PSI: 4)

Do a series of project milestones exist depicting key points and dates in the project?   Y/N

Do these milestones indicate project reviews, requiring project sponsor input?   Y/N

PSI:

Step 3: There Must Be One Leader (Max PSI: 10)

Does the project have a project leader/manager?   Y/N

Does he or she have adequate authority to deliver the project?   Y/N

Has the project manager's authority and responsibility been explicitly defined?   Y/N

Does he or she have the primary responsibility for the planning, implementation, and delivery of the project deliverables?   Y/N

Is this responsibility integrated into his or her performance objectives?   Y/N

Does he or she actively manage/have control of the work of *all* project team members?   Y/N

> *Note:* This control includes the work of those project team members not under direct supervision (e.g., personnel from other departments and contractor companies) and any other contributor (including senior managers) whose work (or lack of work) may/will impact upon the delivery of the project leader's deliverables.

Does a project organization structure clearly define project members roles?   Y/N

PSI:

Step 4: Assign People to Jobs (Max PSI: 10)

10. Resources (PSI: 5)

Does every job in the project plan have a human being's name against it?   Y/N

Where generic names do exist for tasks scheduled for action beyond a 6-to-8-week horizon, is assignment action being taken to resolve generic names into specific human beings?   Y/N

Have project team members been type-categorized (type 1, 2, 3, 4, 5)?   Y/N

Have project assignments been based upon individual strengths and weaknesses?   Y/N

PSI:

11. Resource loading (PSI: 5)

Have resources been phased over time?   Y/N

Has team members' availability to this project been accurately determined?   Y/N

Are team members "day-jobs" taken into account against their scheduled project tasks?   Y/N

Have people been scheduled less that 90% of their available time?   Y/N

Have company, public, and individuals' annual holidays been factored into the project plan—that is, are project members scheduled to be in more than one location or to do more than one task at any one time?   Y/N

PSI:

Step 5: Manage Expectations/Allow a Margin for Error/Have a Fallback Position/Contingency   (Max PSI: 10)

12. Risk management (PSI: 5)

Have all risks to the project been identified?   Y/N

Has the specific risk of departure of key people been analyzed and allowed for?   Y/N

Have all risks been prioritized, based upon their project impact and their probability of occurrence   Y/N

For each risk, is there a risk management action to overcome, mitigate, or avoid?   Y/N

Are risk management actions appropriate to manage the risk and attain the goal?   Y/N

Have the risk management actions/contingent tasks been entered into the WBS?   Y/N

PSI:

13. Manage client/customer expectations (PSI: 3)

Have different project plan options (flavors) been developed in anticipation of negotiations with the project's client (i.e., customer or management)?   Y/N

Can the various project options developed deliver the project goals?   Y/N

Have the different project options been negotiated with the project stakeholders and has sign-off been achieved regarding the project option?   Y/N

PSI:

14. Backup plan/contingency/margin for error (PSI: 2)

Has contingency been planned to manage/address a job running overtime, a QA failure, a missed or late deliverable, and a dependency mismatch?   Y/N

Has the effect of adding more people been factored into the project plan?   Y/N

PSI:

Step 6: Manage With an Appropriate Leadership Style (PSI: 10)]

Since this is not a review of the project manager or his or her performance, the project manager can either (a) rate this out of 10 or (b) give it a nominal value that, again, the project manager will either choose or agree with.

15. Trust placed in each project team member (PSI: 5)

Has the project manager defined the trust he or she places in each team member?   Y/N

Has the project manager defined the management style/requirement necessary for each team member? Y/N

PSI:

16. The ETP "lazy project manager" style (PSI: 5)

Does the project manager include in his or her personal work calendar or diary the management tasks and time required to appropriately manage each team member? Y/N

Does the project manager adopt/operate a dynamic management style? Y/N

PSI:

Step 7: Know What Is Going On (PSI: 10)

17. Using the project plan as instrumentation (PSI: 4)

Does the project manager's daily work practice include checking on tasks starting, tasks finishing, and tasks in progress? Y/N

Does the project manager use the PM tool to record daily progress on current project jobs / tasks? Y/N

Does the project manager daily seek, explode, and complete the detailed planning of project tasks coming into focus in the next 6–8 weeks into single person-day tasks? Y/N

Does the project manager routinely categorize the status of the project (e.g., by color code—red = in trouble; blue = no plan exists, amber = some problems, green = on target)? Y/N

18. Project monitoring/tracking and control (PSI: 3)

Is what the plan says should be happening reflected in the project? Y/N

Is what is happening on the project reflected in the plan? Y/N

Are there "positive signs" on the project? (See [1] for a list of these.) Y/N

Are there "negative signs" on the project? (Again, see [1].) Y/N

Is there a change control management process within the project? Y/N

Comparing actual to plan, give a percentage completion figure for the project. _____

Give the current time behind planned schedule for the project.
_____

19. **Project deliverables (PSI: 3)**

Project Deliverables (as per Project Spec)	Target Date	Achieved (Y/N)	If No—What Was Achieved?
Note: Project deliverables refer to actual results that will deliver business benefits not activities.			

Step 8: Tell People What's Going On (Max PSI: 10)

20. **Project reporting (PSI: 10)**

Do project status reports issue weekly?   Y/N

Are they properly structured or just a rambling account of the week?   _____

Are the status reports issued to the team?   Y/N

Are the status reports issued to the customer?   Y/N

Are the status reports issued to the management?   Y/N

Do the status reports contain historical information or are they just snapshots in time?   _____

Do people read the status reports?   Y/N

How often is project performance reported on in terms of business benefits?   _____

Step 9: Repeat Steps (1) Through (8) Until Step (10) (Max PSI: 10)

21. **The unfolding of the project. (Answers here may cause a rethink in previous PSI scores.)**

Was the goal of the project clear from the outset?   Y/N

If not, when did it become clear?   _____

Was there a document that described the goal at that time?

Y/N

Can we have it?   _____

Were there any significant changes to the goal after that?   Y/N

How many?   _____

Were these changes properly controlled and were plans adjusted accordingly?   Y/N

Did all the stakeholders know where they stood all the time?

Y/N

Was there a proper plan at the outset of the project?

Y/N

Was the plan maintained as time progressed?

Y/N

Did the project always have a project manager?

Y/N

Who?   _____

Did the project manager change since the project started?   Y/N

What was the amount of project management required on the project?   _____

How was this calculated?   _____

Did the project manager have sufficient time available to run the project?   Y/N

Did the project manager take proper ownership of the project?

Y/N

Was project demand (work to be done) matched to supply (people to do the work)?   Y/N

Was this done at the beginning of the project?   Y/N

Was it maintained over its life to date?   Y/N

How do you know?   _____

Did the project plan have contingency in it?   Y/N

Was this used?   Y/N

Was there enough?   Y/N

PSI:

22. Top three priority project issues for resolution

1.

2.

3.

23. Project planning probability of success indicator (PSI)

Goal PSI: (20 max)	Project score:
List of jobs (20 max)	Project score:
One project leader (10 max)	Project score:
Resources assignment (10 max)	Project score:
Managing expectations/contingency/ margin for error (10 max)	Project score:

Total project planning PSI score:

Leadership style (10 max)	Project score:
Monitoring/control (10 max)	Project score:
Reporting (10 max)	Project score:

Total project implementation PSI score:

Total project PSI :

24. Progress to date and planned

Assuming they are available or can be calculated, take the planned and actual progress for the last few months (progress could be measured in, say, earned value or in effort units). Look to see whether the actual progress to date is a slow-climbing line with progress suddenly becoming blazingly fast "next month." If this pattern repeats itself several times, then this is further confirmation that the project has problems.

25. Any other relevant issues

Sometimes the suckers (projects, I mean!) just go ballistic; they go wildly off the rails. Then you need to have a way of understanding what happened, sorting them out, and putting them back on track.

6 Rescuing Projects: Rescuing = Assessing + Scoping and Planning (Steps 1–10)

Questions

? Q.1 A trainee has joined your project team. What is the best leadership style to use?

(a) Leave 'em to it and see whether they sink or swim.

(b) Micromanagement.

(c) Ask another member of the team to take the rookie under his or her wing.

(d) Not your problem. Ask personnel to provide a training plan, and until the new recruit is "up to speed" it's personnel's problem.

? Q.2 You've got a superstar on your project—highly skilled, experienced, motivated, as described earlier in this book. You try to

101

spend a chunk of time every day with him or her. Your rationale is that:

(a) Your spending time with this person inspires him or her and squeezes all the available "superstardom" out of him or her.

(b) Your spending time with him or her serves to advance the project.

(c) You like being with him or her because you can have interesting discussions on the industry area in which you're both involved.

(d) You've nothing better to do.

？ Q.3 Your project has 10 people working on it full time and will run for a year. It has a flat organization structure (i.e., all 10 people report directly to you). How much project management effort will this require from you?

(a) It's a full-time job.

(b) You could run two of these.

(c) You have two and a half days a week available to do jobs on the project.

(d) You have four days a week available to do jobs on the project.

Answers

Q.1
(a) 0 points: Lots of people do, but it ain't the right answer.
(b) 5 points: Yessiree. No question.
(c) 2 points: Two points if you've assumed that the mentor will do the micromanagement. Five if you've built it into your plan.
(d) 0 points: Come off it!

Q.2
(a) 0 points: My God—you're some egomaniac!
(b) 0 points: Oh no it doesn't. With these kind of people the project would be advancing whether you intervened or not.
(c) 5 points: By all means. Just don't fool yourself into thinking that this is time spent "doing project management."
(d) 5 points: I like this one. If you've literally got nothing better to do, then your project is under control. Isn't it?

Q.3
(a) 5 points: It certainly is. Send me an e-mail, and I'll do the calculation for you.
(b) 0 points: Not unless your other name is Clark Kent.
(c) 0 points: You don't.
(d) 0 points: You don't.

Scores

12–15 points: Good enough. This is the kind of standard we're coming to expect.

10 points: Sloppy, sloppy. Come on, we're six chapters into the book, and there's a whole heap more to go. Concentrate.

Less than 10: You didn't really mean to give those answers, did you? Go back to the start and do it again.

Introduction

When a project goes off the rails we can think of it as in Figure 6.1.

Figure 6.1 Project rescues.

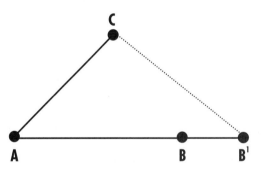

The project depicted in Figure 6.1 was meant to go from A to B. It actually went someplace different—to C. Your job now is to do the following.

1. Figure out why it went to C.

2. Figure out where it must now go, given that time has moved on since the project was launched. In Figure 6.1, this is called B^1.

3. Do a plan to go from C to B^1.

You now have all the skills to do these steps, described as follows:

1. Figure out why it went to C—use the assessing projects in Chapter 5.

2. Figure out where it must now go, given that time has moved on since the project was launched. In Figure 6.1, this is called B^1—use scoping projects in Chapter 2.

3. Do a plan to go from C to B^1—use making plans in Chapter 2. You can also use Chapter 4—or somebody else can—to assess your resulting plan.

Shortest chapter so far!

Project management is about predicting the future and then trying to make what you said would happen, happen. One of the few ways you can improve your ability to do these rather scary things is to audit completed projects—successful or otherwise. That's what we do here.

7 Auditing Completed Projects (Steps 1–10)

Questions

? Q.1 Assuming that you use your project plan as your road map through the project, how often should you update it?

(a) Every day.

(b) Constantly.

(c) Once a week.

(d) Not at all. Now that the powers-that-be—the management, customer, standards people—have approved the plan, the real fun starts.

? Q.2 You get a monumental (bad, needless to add) surprise on your project. What do you do?

(a) Punish the perpetrator.

(b) Point out to the perpetrator the impact of what he or she has done, help him or her to put a plan in place to fix the problem, and micromanage him or her out of it.

(c) Do nothing to the perpetrator. It's your job as project manager to deal with these things.

(d) Vow to put more contingency in the plan next time.

? Q.3 Things are going swimmingly on your project. You've never seen a plan come together so well before. There are only a few weeks left. You think you'll fit in a well-earned vacation. What do you do next?

(a) Call your travel agent and book it.

(b) Forget the whole idea.

(c) Do (a) plus nominate a member of the team as your deputy while you're gone.

(d) Book it for when the project ends.

Answers

Q.1
(a) 5 points: Yep. Among other things this gives you an early warning system whose maximum window is 24 hours. A reassuring feeling, I would have thought.
(b) 5 points: Or this. This is what I would do.
(c) 2 points: Ho-hum. It's better than nothing.
(d) 0 points: Now, come on, you knew you weren't going to get away with that.

Q.2
(a) 0 points: Nope. And if that's the culture of your organization, I suggest you begin looking for a new job.
(b) 5 points: Absolutely. You may not be very popular with the perpetrator, he or she may never thank you for it, but it's the way to go.
(c) 0 points: No, it's not. Or to be more precise, it's not your job to build a plan that holds in all circumstances. This is the same as (a) except that instead of punishing the perpetrator, you punish yourself.
(d) 5 points: This is a vow that I think every project manager should take on being appointed to the role.

Q.3
(a) 0 points: Be very, very afraid. A healthy insecurity is a good trait to have in a project manager.
(b) 0 points: Not a good idea. Rest and relaxation is vital to your well-being.

(c) 1 point: Be very afraid.
(d) 5 points: And enjoy it. When you come back they'll want you to play the game again. Only this time for bigger stakes.

Scores

15 points: Not too hard to get a high score here.

12–14 points: You should have gotten top marks here.

Less than 12: I don't know how you did it.

Introduction

If you don't realize what mistakes you made previously, you will make those mistakes again. If you don't understand what things you did that worked last time, then you won't necessarily do those things again.

To ensure that you work out what the good, the bad, and the ugly were on any completed project, you should do some form of audit or postmortem. The audit should be a compulsory last job on any project and in any project work breakdown structure.

Here is how I would go about doing one:

1. Tell everybody who was involved in the project—team, customer, management, and any other stakeholders—that you are doing a postmortem to round out the project. Ask them for a contribution. Tell them you want them to be blunt and that all the submissions will be gathered together into a final document that will be published. Those inside the company will get the whole document; those outside will get a version that has had any stuff confidential to your company removed. (This latter device allows you to involve the customer, subcontractors, or any other outside organizations but still be the final arbiter of what goes to them.) Participation is optional and anonymity is allowed.

2. Give them some simple guidelines:

   - You're expecting 1–3 pages.

   - Essentially you want them to write a "how was it for you?" essay. You want them to give their story of the project.

   - They should give both positives and negatives—what was done well, what was done badly.

- You're particularly interested in any rules of thumb or other estimating-type data that may be of value to other members of the team.

- Ask them to list the three key lessons they would take away from the project.

- Give them a closing date for submissions.

3. In the meantime, you write an objective account of the project. Write it like a police report. Confine yourself to the facts and keep your own opinions out of it. If you like, you can also write a "how was it for you?" essay, but make clear which is which and the difference between the two.

4. When all your material is in, gather it together, generate the version from outside the organization, publish, and be damned.

5. You might also like to put the estimating data into some central repository where everyone can access it. If this is the first time this has ever been done, make a big song and dance about it—your organization's historical project database has just been born.

6. Ensure that somebody does something as a result of the audit (e.g., an improvement project is put in place, or a single improvement is made or the top three suggestions are acted on or something). Don't just let the audit gather dust.

An example of the "police report"–type document is given in the User Assistance section.

User assistance

Introduction

This document is an audit on the XYZ project, undertaken by ABC Company, which began its acceptance test in December 1993. There are two sections in the document.

Section 1 tells the story of the project from start to finish and contains statistics about the project. Section 2 gives a series of general recommendations that our ABC Company could usefully implement.

Appendix A contains accounts of the project written by all of those involved (not included here).

I would recommend that the document be circulated as widely as possible within our ABC Company and that a list of actions, arising from the document, be drawn up.

The story of the project

Introduction

This project began on Monday, May 17, and ended on Friday, December 17, a total elapsed time of seven months. It consumed 1,600 person-days of effort (about seven person-years) and produced approximately 60,000 lines of code. The aim of the project was to deliver versions of APRODUCT and BPRODUCT, which had been modified to operate with XYZ's database. A version of CPRODUCT, also operating on XYZ's database, was included within the scope of the project.

The project underwent a major change shortly after the contract was agreed so that what was in the original proposal bore little relationship to what was finally done. The change was this:

> The original proposal from ABC to XYZ said that a DPRODUCT product development project was in progress and that the XYZ would involve taking this DPRODUCT product at some point in its development and replacing the DPRODUCT database with the database.

There was, in fact, no product development project in progress and so, the XYZ *actually* involved implementing *both* of the following.

- Those areas of APRODUCT and BPRODUCT required for the XYZ pilot;

- The link to the database.

In terms of size this meant that the project went from being a 455-MD project to a 1,600-MD project.

That we were able to deliver with no slip on our side, despite such a major change of scope was due primarily to two slips of a month each on the XYZ side. If these had not occurred, we would have had to ask for changes to the deadline. As it was, the changes to the scope remained completely transparent to XYZ and their other suppliers, and as far as they were concerned we merely implemented our original proposal.

This two-month slip was our good luck. The bad luck was that we lost a month on the design, which, in different circumstances, we need not have done.

The individual phases of the project are summarized on an estimating score card and discussed in the following sections. Based on the time-sheet analysis, the project was achieved with comparatively little late night or weekend working—by and large people worked 160 or so hours per month.

Overall

The original (17 May) estimates of effort and schedule for the project were 455 MD and a completion date of 18 October respectively. These were realistic estimates that we were confident we could achieve.

When the scope of the project changed on 2 July, these estimates no longer had any basis in reality. What we then said was that for us to have any chance of meeting the 18 October delivery date, we would basically have to put everyone in ABC onto the project. This is what we did, and this gave us a revised project size of 850 MD. This was not a realistic estimate nor was it any kind of an attempt to produce one. It was merely a statement of the available person-days, and despite doing this, the 18 October delivery date still looked like being well nigh impossible. We did not tell XYZ or their other suppliers any of this.

Around mid August, when it looked like we would not meet the deadline and would have to come clean, a slip of a month occurred on the XYZ side. This gave us a new delivery date of 15 November, which implied a new effort estimate of 1,100 MD. Again this was not a realistic estimate; it was merely a statement of the new level of person-days made available by the slip. While this slip made the project significantly more possible, the estimate was still a driven-by-the-end-date estimate rather than a realistic one.

A second XYZ slip of a month occurred on 28 September. One of the results of this was that, for the first time since the scope had changed, we were in a position to do a realistic estimate for the project. We did this and calculated effort and schedule values of 1,250 MD and a delivery date of 29 November, respectively.

In the estimating score card (see Table 7.1), I have treated these as the first realistic estimates for the project, and have compared the actuals against these.

Phase by phase

Design
This has been described in a separate memo. We estimated the effort pretty much correctly but lost a month on the elapsed time.

Code and unit test
Effort underestimated by about 20%.

Integration
Effort underestimated by nearly 20%.

Alpha test
Amount of work involved in bug fixing was *seriously* underestimated. See also bug statistics.

Table 7.1   Estimating Scorecard

Phase	Estimated Schedule (months)	% Effort (MD)	Actual % Schedule (months)	%Effort (MD)	Differences Schedule (months)	% Effort (MD)
Design	1.5	220	2.5	225	1	5
Code and unit test	2	450	2	540	0	90
Integration	1	110	1	130	0	20
Alpha test	1	320	1	600	0	280
System delivery	0	0	0.25	20	0.25	20
Support	6.5	50	6.5	60	0	10
Project management	6.5	100	6.5	84	0	16
Totals		1,250		1,659		409

System delivery
This was a big success. It was done in a week; the system worked really well because it had been so well-tested here; and following the week, no bugs were reported.

Support
Underestimated by 20%.

Project management
Overestimated by 16%.

Note that in general, there is a tendency here to underestimate the effort involved in everything. The 20% figure was also encountered on another ABC project.

Things the company could usefully do

Design audit

If the product/database pilot software is to be used as a basis for further development here, I think it is essential that a design audit be performed on the existing software, before any further work is done on it.

Software process improvement

In terms of the Software Engineering Institute (SEI) software process maturity model, the company is probably somewhere between levels 1 and 2. The following are things it could do to begin moving it definitely out of level 1 through level 2 to level 3, which is the level at which it could seek ISO 9001 certification.

Level 1 (initial)—level 2 (repeatable)

- Commitments: Document existing system.

- Planning: Document existing system; train people.

- Configuration management: Crucial that company either hires somebody with experience in this area or else trains somebody. The existing system needs to be formalized and documented.

- Quality assurance: Start an ISO 9001 program.

Level 2 (repeatable)—Level 3 (defined)

- Standards: Determine standards needed; implement and document them.

- Software inspections: Implement these as a matter of urgency.

- Testing: Formalize and document the method.

- Advanced configuration management: Extend the existing system if necessary.

- Process models and architecture: Define, implement, and document a process.

- Software engineering process group: Continue ISO 9001 program.

Training required

From what I have seen on this project, the following are areas where training of staff is required:

- Analysis and design (use of a standard method);

- Configuration management;

- Project management (use of standard method);

- Time management, self-organization, estimating, and scheduling.

Happily, running multiple projects can be made only marginally more complicated than running one. Here's how.

8 Running Multiple Projects

Questions

? Q.1 You are a project management consultant called in to do a rescue. The project is many months past its delivery date and still going strong, burning up money like there's no tomorrow. The project has all sorts of specs and other documentation, a harassed project manager sweating over a vast Gantt chart, people working all the hours God sends, meetings, status reports, and all the other paraphernalia of a project. It's like ancient Egypt during the construction of the great pyramid of Cheops. You do a quick PSI calculation and come out with a 25. How is this possible, given that, this late in the project, you'd expect it to be much higher?

(a) It's a trick question, and I've fed you misinformation.

(b) The people are working overtime.

(c) There is no change control.

(d) The status reporting is inadequate.

? Q.2 Your project has gone ballistic. You come out with your hands up and admit everything. You go through a few days that would make a weekend in hell seem like an attractive proposition. The powers that be—somewhat hesitantly—express their confidence in you and ask you to plan the way forward. You brainstorm the new plan with the team and then get stuck in over a hot project planning tool to build the plan. Next day—before you have it all anywhere near ready—your boss comes along. He or she has just spoken to a few of the team members, and they claim to have no idea what they should be doing. They are also making noises about you having "lost touch with the project" as you sit in your office, clogging up the color printer with Gantt charts. Your boss angrily reminds you what it's costing the company for the team to have its wheels spinning while you work on the plan. (He or she uses a more colorful—three-word—expression than "work on"! Perhaps he or she also utters the classic "We don't have time to plan—just do the work!") Do you:

(a) Basically tell him or her that you're sorry; this is what happened before; and you're not going to make the same mistake again. Nobody goes anywhere until the plan is written, presented, and approved.

(b) Drop everything, go out, round up the troops, and start working.

(c) Resign.

(d) Tell him or her something calming and then go out and give the team an earful about loyalty and reporting structures.

? Q.3 True or false. A project will go wrong if its demand (work to be done) and supply (people to do the work) aren't the same.

(a) True.

(b) False.

(c) Things aren't as simple as that. The question rules out issues like motivation, levels of experience, and so on.

(d) You can always work overtime and make the equation come right.

Answers

Q.1
(a) 0 points: You wish.
(b) 0 points: I'll bet they are, but that's not the right answer.

(c) 5 points: That'll do it every time. With no fixed goal, it is impossible to fix the list of jobs, and after that it all goes to hell.
(d) 0 points: I'm sure it is, but that's not the right answer, either.

Q.2

(a) 5 points: You guessed it. (Or hopefully, you weren't guessing but actually knew.)
(b) 0 points: You only said that to upset me—tell me you did.
(c) 1 point: Sure you could, but it's hardly an answer, is it?
(d) 1 point: They probably wouldn't give a damn, but it might make you feel better.

Q.3

(a) 5 points: Sure is.
(b) 0 points: Sure isn't.
(c) 0 points: I think things are as simple as that.
(d) 5 points: The statement is true. Whether the overtime (additional supply) will be enough to balance the equation (meet the demand) is a separate question.

Scores

15 points: Good.

11 points: Okay.

Less than 11: Maybe you'll do better in Part Two.

Introduction

Running one project is bad enough. Running many at the same time seems to get everyone in a terrible flap. It needn't. If you are responsible for multiple projects, this is one of those rare occasions in life where the whole is indeed equal to the sum of the parts—with two provisos.

First, you need to separate this project from all the others by precisely bounding its goal. Then you need to take into account people's availability. Apart from these two issues, the projects can be treated completely independently of each other, and the 10 steps applied to each in turn.

In this chapter we present some tools for managing multiple projects and getting a handle on people's availability. These tools are the following:

- The organization-wide supply and demand;

- Organization-wide project assignment;

- Personal dance cards.

As usual, in the User Assistance section, we present examples of all of these things.

Organization-wide supply and demand

I once came across a man who had this problem. He ran a customer support organization, providing both telephone and on-site support. He had 17 people. His customers were never happy with the level of service they received. His people were either approaching burn-out, going through it, or already out the far side and getting ready for their next one (burn-out, I mean). Their lives were a constant tale of late nights, working weekends, and priorities changed at a minute's notice. He said he needed help with "prioritizing tasks."

We did a simple calculation. In a week, how many person-days did he have available to him? Seventeen times five days equals 85 person-days (maximum, assuming full strength and 100% efficiency).

Now, in a typical week, how many person-days worth of requests might end up on his desk? We looked at the last few weeks. The average was coming in around 200.

With supply = 85 and demand = 200, you have the recipe for a short and unhappy life. To be "prioritizing tasks" in such circumstances was tantamount to rearranging the deck chairs on the *Titanic*.

The organization-wide supply and demand calculation is the first step to putting yourself in a position to run multiple projects. Quite simply, it figures out how much work is to be done and whether there are enough people to do that work. If the organization-wide supply and demand calculation isn't right, you can forget the rest. See the User Assistance section for a fully worked example.

Organization-wide project assignment

A request I have heard many times is the manager of multiple projects asking whether it is possible to feed all of the projects and all of the people into a software tool like MS Project. The idea is that this would then give the manager overall command and control and a total view of his or her organization, its projects, and its people.

I'm sure such a thing is technically feasible. I'm sure the good folks at Microsoft could tell us how. The only problem is that, in my experience, I've never seen it work. Even assuming the thing can be created in the first place, I think it would quickly go out of date due to no/partial/inaccurate updating.

Still, the truth is you need to have such a view. In my opinion, our old buddy the spreadsheet does just fine on that score. The User Assistance section gives a worked example.

Personal dance cards

Whether you noticed or not, the previous spreadsheet was dependent on people knowing their own availability. If I am planning my project, and you are going to work on my project, I need to know whether that is full-time or part-time, and if the latter, exactly what that translates into in terms of hours per day, days per week, or days per month.

You could argue that people know that. I would argue that they almost invariably don't, and, in fact, the situation is a good deal worse than that because of the following effect that often occurs, an effect that shows that sometimes by trying to help people, you can really mess them up.

Let's say you're going to work on my project. I ask you what your availability is. You show me something like the following:

- Project X: Two days per week;

- Project Y: One-half day per week;

- Support: One-half day per week;

- Available: Two days per week.

Fair enough. However, then you say—all in the spirit of trying to help me and do the best you can for me—"Project X is winding down, and even though I'm planned to work on it two days per week, it won't take as much as that. I'd say you could have one of those two days."

Now I'm also trying to help the person for whom I'm planning the project, and I never have enough supply available to me. Now, here, out of nowhere, some supply has magically appeared. Will I take it? You bet I will. I'll certainly be sorely tempted to. The trouble is it's a mirage, and if you build part of your plan around it, there's a good chance you will come to grief.

To get over the problem, we have come up with the idea of "dance cards." (The reference is to that more genteel time when ladies at dances had cards, and if gentlemen wanted to dance with a particular lady, they wrote their names in particular slots on the dance card. In other words, the ladies took bookings.) Dance cards allow you to book your time against various projects. In particular, they stop you from double booking.

In the User Assistance section we show you an example.

User assistance

Organization-wide supply and demand

Table 8.1 shows an organization-wide supply and demand calculation for the Acme Corporation. There is slightly more demand than supply, about 5%. From Table 8.1, we can learn the following.

1. If nothing was going to change in this organization over the next year, they could probably live with this.

2. Assuming that there will be change, then provided the person running the organization remained conscious of the delicate supply-demand balance, there wouldn't be a problem. Very precisely, what I mean by this last statement is that, provided that every time new demand is added (the organization is asked to undertake new projects) or supply is reduced (through people leaving) the organization recalculates the

Table 8.1   ACME Corporation Supply/Demand for 1998

Demand in 1998		
Project	Basis	Person-months
Largo 3.3	900 MD	45
Largo 4.1	One-third the size of 3.3	15
Relish 3.5.09	Two people for two months	4
Relish 3.6	Two people for two months	4
Bronze 4.0	Two full-time for three months; two part-time for three months	8.4
Bronze 5.0	Two full-time for three months; two part-time for three months	8.4
EMU	140 MM	140
Y2K	295 days	15
Reporting	2.5 people × three months	7.5
Modeling	Four months; one person	4
DEFROST development	1	1
Lance development	1	1
SMOG development	1	1
Support	Four people full-time	48
		302.3
Supply in 1998	21 people × 12 months	252
	5.5 × 11	60.5
	Less annual leave	27
		285.5

supply-demand equation and acts sensibly on the basis of the result. Note that this is "change control" in action.

3. The ideal position for such an organization is to have the supply slightly in excess of the demand. This then gives the organization some contingency to deal with the unexpected. This is not to say that there are a bunch of people hanging around waiting for something to happen. What's more likely is that each individual project would have its own piece of contingency. This would mean that the effect of events like, say,

people leaving, could be localized in that particular project, while new projects could be treated as exactly that—a new project that would be planned and resourced properly as described in the opening chapters of this book.

Organization-wide project assignment

Table A (in the color section of this book) shows an organization-wide project assignment for the Acme Corporation.

The top part of Table A shows the following:

- The projects being worked on;

- When these projects run;

- Who's working on them;

- Those people's availability requirement on the project (i.e., the project plans for those projects are based on the availabilities shown on the spreadsheet). The number "1" means full time, "0.4" means two days out of every five, and so on.

Turning to the bottom part of Table A, we find the following:

- The "who" column shows that person's monthly availability to the organization. Each individual cell in the bottom part of Table A shows if there are any problems in terms of that person's availability. A few examples follow.

- JG is available full-time every month. The only project on which JG is required to work is the "department management" project. Thus, by subtracting the monthly demand of the various projects (in this case, one) from the monthly availability, we find out whether or not there is an oversupply or shortfall problem with JG. In this case, there isn't.

- Now let's look at POC. He or she is available full-time. However, he or she is committed full-time to two projects—Largo and Reporting. Again, the spreadsheet subtracts the monthly demand of both of these projects from the monthly availability giving a shortfall (represented by the minus) of 1. Clearly, this won't wash.

- However, there is also some oversupply. RSV is available two days per week in January (0.4), so maybe he or she can be used to fix part of the problem—or maybe there's no point in putting him or her on for a month only to move on to something else, or maybe RSV doesn't have the right skill set. The spreadsheet makes it easy for the organization manager to consider these different scenarios.

To update the spreadsheet shown in Table A, do the following.

- For a new or changed project, in the top half of the spreadsheet (Table A):

  · Put in/change the project.

  · Put in/change the people working on it and the availability that is expected of them.

- In the bottom half of the spreadsheet (Table A), change the formula so that all of a person's project demands are subtracted from his or her availability.

The result will be that you will see oversupply or shortfall at a glance.

Finally, as you would expect, perceived oversupply becomes greater as the spreadsheet goes further off into the future. This is only because projects are ending, and new projects have not yet been identified to take their places.

Personal dance card

Table 8.2 shows a simple dance card that you can tailor further, if you wish. This one, however, contains all the essential elements.

- The dance card covers a six-week period.

- All of the owner's projects are written down the left-hand side.

- A calculation is made in the "basis" and "total" columns of the total effort involved in these projects over this period. Note that this is an *estimate*.

Table 8.2   Personal Dance Card

#	Project	Basis		Total	Actuals — This Month (Hrs)						This Week (Hrs)				
					22/01	29/01	05/02	12/02	19/02	26/02	M	T	W	T	F
1	Group project	1.5	dpw	9	8.5	7.5					2.5	1.5	2	1.5	1.5
2	SB/software	1.5	dpw	9	10	10					2.5	2	1	2.5	2
3	Other subsidiaries	0.75	dpw	4.5	1.5	5						1.5	2	0.5	1
4	Product development project	1	dpw	6	1.5	2					2				
5	ISO	1	dpw	6	11	3									
6	Administration	0.75	dpw	4.5	8.5	7					1.5	1.5	11.5	1	1.5
7	Training others	0	dpw	0											
8	Personal training/appraisal	0	dpw	0	1										
9	SSPMW	0.05	dpw	0.3	0.5	0.5					0.5				
10	Holidays		days												
	Sales meeting/sales support					7						2	0.5	2	2.5
				39.3	42.5	42					9	8.5	8	8	8.5
		Extra hours			2.5	2									
	Number of weeks	6													

- On the right-hand side the dance card has areas for recording actual hours every day and accumulating these into actual hours per week.

- Thus, using a dance card, people can see where their time really goes, how much time is actually going into certain projects, and how much time might be available for other projects.

In *Working Knowledge* [6], the authors quote Hewlett-Packard CEO Lew Platt as saying, "If HP knew what HP knows, we would be three times as profitable." This chapter describes how to know what you know.

9 Building a Historical Database (Knowledge Management)

Questions

Q.1 How often should you update the plan?

(a) Never.

(b) Only if you have to renegotiate the contract.

(c) Daily.

(d) Weekly.

Q.2 You're a software or IT project manager. Your company has no historical data from previously completed projects. Your boss comes back from a conference and tells you that from now on, you need to "gather metrics" from your projects and build "a historical database." What do you do?

(a) Get out those old database design books from college and call Oracle to get license pricing.

(b) Buy a copy of Boehm's *Software Engineering Economics* [7] and begin to gather the 15 elements of metrics data described in Part IVB of that book.

(c) Jot down on a piece of paper the distribution of effort and elapsed time over the phases of a project you're currently working on.

(d) Say "sure" but do nothing. It's just another boss fad.

❥ Q.3   Same scenario as question 2. Why is gathering metrics such a good idea?

(a) It'll improve your estimating.

(b) It'll shorten time to market.

(c) It will reduce the risk of your projects going out of control.

(d) It'll keep your boss happy.

Answers

Q.1

(a) 5 points: Okay, this is something of a trick question. I believe that there are actually two plans—the contractual one and the operational one. Think of the contractual one as the one that is appended to the legal project contract. If it were to happen that you didn't have to renegotiate the contract over the life of the project, then the contractual plan would never change. On the basis that this was what you meant when you gave this answer, score five. (It was what you meant, wasn't it? If it wasn't, score zero.)

(b) 5 points: Provided it's the contractual plan you're talking about.

(c) 5 points: The operational one, yes.

(d) 3 points: I'd prefer daily, but it's better than nothing.

Q.2

(a) 0 points: Now you knew that wasn't the right answer. We've been pretty lenient in Part One of the book. You won't find us so forgiving in the next part.

(b) 1 point: It's a great book, but I can almost guarantee you'll never use them.

(c) 5 points: As a first step, it's unimpeachable. Try it and see what a quick win you get with it.

(d) 0 points: Yes, bosses can be faddy. But some "fads" actually turn out

to be quite good things. Take the quality movement, for example. This fad is a good one. Ignore it at your peril.

Q.3
(a) 5 points: It will.
(b) 5 points: It will. By understanding where the time and effort went in say a design phase, you can look for ways to shorten the phase, through things like prototyping, rapid application development, and fancier tools.
(c) 5 points: It will.
(d) 5 points: It will. (I told you it was a good fad!)

Scores

15 points: That wasn't hard to do, now was it?

13–14 points: Write out 20 times "metrics are a good fad!"

Less than 13: Maybe you didn't understand the questions.

Introduction

Projects are about predicting the future and making that prediction come true. If that's your business, then your surest aid to getting it right is to learn from previous projects. In this chapter we talk about gathering the data to give you the information you need—in short, knowledge management.

When I began this chapter, I was of two minds—whether to give it a very simple title, "Keeping Records," for example, or a very fancy title. In the end I chose the fancy one—both publishers and public seem to prefer that—but my heart is still with the simple one.

The danger with the fancy titles—"historical database," "knowledge management"—is that people immediately assume you are going to get into some brand of rocket science. Someday in the future, you may indeed want to get into something like that, and then there are plenty of people out there to get into it with you.

My intention here is much more modest. It is to show you that by recording some very basic information, all of which you either already have or can generate easily, you give yourself some very powerful capabilities. Try it on even one project and you'll inevitably see what I mean.

Data

First you need to capture the basic data. You do this by updating the plan religiously as we have previously described. Then, by the time the project ends, you will have a description of how the project actually unfolded. You will have the actual chaining together of all the jobs, along with some or all of the following:

- The amount of work each job actually took;
- The actual dependencies between jobs;
- Who did what job;
- What those peoples' availabilities were over the life of the project;
- How long the job took;
- The cost of the job;
- Any assumptions relevant to the job;
- Perhaps other noteworthy information (e.g., unexpected things that happened).

You can now use this data to generate some useful information.

An additional step that is not particularly time-consuming and that I believe would be well worthwhile would be to take a weekly PSI of the project and record these figures in a spreadsheet.

Information

In my opinion, there are three kinds of information you need:

- High-level estimates and actuals;
- Templates for projects;
- Project performance information.

High-level estimates and actuals

To gather these, do the following:

1. As a first step, calculate how the effort and elapsed time were distributed over the major phases of the project.

2. Calculate both the actual amount (effort in, for example, person-days, and elapsed time in, for example, weeks or months) and the amount as a percentage of the total.

3. As a further refinement of this you can then break down particular phases for a next level of detail.

4. See Table 7.1 for an estimating scorecard, a simple form that enables you to do this.

Templates for projects

If you have captured the data described in the preceding Data section, you now have a much improved starting point for your next project. The next time you won't be starting with a blank sheet of paper.

An example of such a template, derived from ETP's Silver Bullet software product, is given in this chapter's User Assistance section.

Project performance information

The weekly PSI data will enable you to see at a glance—particularly, if you graph it—how your project fared over its life. By capturing these "project vital signs" on a weekly basis, you will have kept your finger very finely on the pulse of the project. While the detailed history may already fast be becoming a blur, the key events that happened and that shaped the project will be immediately apparent and recognizable.

Knowledge

Using the basic data gathered, having converted that into information as described, you can now use it to make comparisons, make connections between projects, and anticipate consequences. Note, for example, the following:

• Using templates you can build project plans much more quickly and be more sure of their basis in reality.

- You can compare the distribution of effort and elapsed time on a proposed project with that of previous projects and draw inferences.

- As the PSI graph or profile of a project starts to unroll, you can see how it compares with other projects and ensure that you do not fall into traps you may have fallen into on those projects.

All of this enables you to distill your project planning and management skill and experience into a compact, highly portable, easily accessible, easy-to-read "database" of knowledge. If you don't have more successful projects as a result of this, I'll eat my hat.

User assistance

Table 9.1 contains a piece of the kind of template we talked about earlier. The estimates on which the tasks in Table 9.1 are based are listed in Table 9.2.

Table 9.1   Template for Software Development Project

ID	Task Name	Duration	Work	Start	Finish	Predecessors	Resource Names
1	1 Product requirement documents	26.25 days	28.5 dasy	14 December 1998	19 January 1999		
2	1.1 Research user requirements	10.5 days	7 days	14 December 1998	28 December 1998		
3	1.1.1 Gather info on competitive products	0.5 days	0.5 days	14 December 1998	14 December 1998		Analysts
4	1.1.2 Review with marketing	0.5 days	2 days	14 December 1998	14 December 1998	3	Analysts(200%)Marketing(200%)
5	1.1.3 Identify users	0.5 days	0.5 days	15 December 1998	15 December 1998	4	Analysts
6	1.1.4 Prepare user questionnaires	2 days	2 days	15 December 1998	17 December 1998	5	Analysts
7	1.1.5 Distribute questionnaires	0.5 days	0.5 days	17 December 1998	17 December 1998	6	Administrative assistant
8	1.1.6 Retrieve questionnaires	0.5 days	0.5 days	25 December 1998	25 December 1998	7FS+1 wk	Administrative assistant
9	1.1.7 Analysis information	1 day	1 day	25 December 1998	28 December 1998	8	Analysts
10	1.2 Write requirements document	10 days	10 days	28 December 1998	11 January 1999	2	Analysts
11	1.3 Review cycle	5.25 days	11 days	11 January 1999	18 January 1999	10	
12	1.3.1 Circulate	0.5 days	0.5 days	11 January 1999	11 January 1999		Administrative assistant
13	1.3.2 Individual review	0.5 days	2.5 dasy	12 January 1999	12 January 1999	12	Requirements reviewer(500%)
14	1.3.3 Review meeting	0.5 days	3 days	12 January 1999	12 January 1999	13	Analysts, requirements reviewer(500%)
15	1.3.4 Changes to document	3 days	3 days	13 January 1999	15 January 1999	14	Analysts
16	1.3.5 Circulate again	0.5 days	0.5 days	18 January 1999	18 January 1999	15	Administrative assistant
17	1.3.6 Second review	0.25 day	1.5 days	18 January 1999	18 January 1999	16	Analysts, requirements reviewer(500%)
18	1.4 Signoff	0.5 days	0.5 days	18 January 1999	19 January 1999	11	Administrative assistant
19	1.5 Requirements complete	0 days	0 days	19 January 1999	19 January 1999	18	
20	2 Produce system/accpetance test plan	28.75 days	34.5 days	19 January 1999	26 February 1999	1	
21	2.1 Research	5 days	5 days	19 January 1999	26 January 1999		Analysts
22	2.2 Write navigation tests	3 dasy	3 days	26 January 1999	29 January 1999	21	
23	2.2.1 Define last sequence	1 day	1 day	26 January 1999	27 January 1999		Analysts
24	2.2.2 Write test scripts	1 day	1 day	27 January 1999	28 January 1999	23	Analysts
25	2.2.3 Define expected results	1 day	1 day	28 January 1999	29 January 1999	24	Analysts
26	2.3 Write functionality tests	3 days		29 January 1999			
27	2.3.1 Def...						

Table 9.2   Derivation of Estimates in Software Development Project Template

Task Name	Work	Notes
Produce requirements document	28.5d	
Research user requirements	7d	
Gather information on competitive products	0.5d	Review the World Wide Web to see products Review advertisements and literature
Review with marketing	2d	Meeting of four people for 0.5 days Agenda beforehand and minutes afterwards
Identify users	0.5d	Need to identify a population of users from which we want to gather information May need interaction with people
Prepare user questionnaires	2d	Construct a suitable questionnaire
Distribute questionnaires	0.5d	Mail, e-mail, or fax questionnaires
Retrieve questionnaires	0.5d	Assumes a lag of one week prior to retrieving the questionnaires
Analyze information	1d	This prepares us for writing the requirements document
Write requirements document	10d	Assuming document has 10 chapters and we do one chapter per day
Review cycle	11d	
Circulate	0.5d	Half a day's administrative effort
Individual review	2.5d	Based on one week elapsed time and half a day's effort from each of five people
Review meeting	3d	Five people plus the author for half a day elapsed
Changes to document	3d	Author working for one-third the time it took to write the document originally, say three person-days
Circulate again	0.5d	Half a day's administrative effort
Second review	1.5d	Same six people for two hours
Signoff	0.5d	Administrative effort involved in getting signoff
Requirements complete	0d	MILESTONE
Produce system/acceptance test plan	34.5d	Once requirements are complete we can write the system test plan
Research	5d	One week's study of available system documentation by the person who will write the system test plan
Write navigation tests	3d	The definition of all user interface deliverables This includes screen flows, function keys, screen validation, and user interface standards The navigation must consider the profile of users and their computer literacy and expertise in business processes
Define test sequence	1d	
Write test scripts	1d	
Define expected results	1d	

Maybe you have a bunch of project management processes already. How do you know if they're any good?

10 Analyzing Project Management Processes (Steps 1–10)

Questions

? Q.1 You are coming into the closing three months of your project. (At least you think you are.) However, for the second time in a month, the project manager has slipped the end date further into the future. What do you do?

(a) Grin and bear it. We're nearly there, and there's nothing can be done about it now. Make a mental note to include more contingency next time out.

(b) Specify precisely additional, detailed reporting requirements that you'd like to see the project manager include in the project status report.

(c) Declare a state of emergency because the project is now a runaway and send in the rescue squad.

(d) Micromanage the project manager.

❓ Q.2 You have just taken up a new job in a new organization. Its project management is a shambles. That's part of the reason they've hired you—they want you to put it all right for them. One of the first things you zero in on is status reports. They are conspicuous in their absence. You send out an edict saying that you want them from now on, every Friday, say, before close of business. The response is less than enthusiastic. What do you do?

(a) Send the edict out again—worded even more strongly.

(b) Tell your boss and ask him to send out the more strongly worded one over his name.

(c) Publish an overall organization status report, showing each project as a line item. For those for which you don't get status reports, flag them as "status unknown."

(d) Threaten to hold up people's expense claims by the same number of days that their status report is late.

❓ Q.3 Same scenario as the previous question. The status reports start flowing, but quite frankly, they are rubbish—rambling essays about life on the project. You have a picture in your head (or better still, on paper) of precisely what you want. How do you get the troops to give you what you want?

(a) Another edict.

(b) Infiltrate what you want a piece at a time, or even a project at a time. For example, one of the things you want to see is a change history of the project's end date. Ask them to put this in commencing from this week. If you do this repeatedly you should eventually end up with what you want.

(c) Do (b) but ask them to make it retrospective to the beginning of the project.

(d) Run a training course for them in status reporting.

Answers

Q.1

(a) 1 point: Tricky one this. However, this is not the right answer. You get the one point for reminding yourself yet again about the value of contingency. You'd have got two points if, instead of making a mental note, you'd written it down!

(b) 2 points: This is better. The detail you're looking for is the underlying reason why this effect is happening on the project. Get worried if the project manager can't offer an acceptable insight into what this is. As your checklist for getting this insight, refer to the section on "Why projects fail" in Chapter 1.

(c) 4 points: The only reason I haven't given you five is because it might be premature. On the other hand, in weeks to come you might regret you hadn't taken this action.

(d) 5 points: This one works best for me—but I wouldn't get too upset if you wanted to score them differently. The way I think of it is that the project manager is a bit like a subcontractor to you. You can think of the project he or she is running as part of the overall project that is your job. If he or she is not giving you the level of service you had expected, then that's your justification for wading in. You might combine this with answer (b), and let things run for another week or, at most, two. Then if things are still looking dodgy, go to answer (c).

Q.2

(a) 5 points: I've come to the conclusion that a four-point approach works well in situations like this. If you like watching police shows on TV, then you'll be familiar with the four-point approach. It basically goes like this:

- *Announcement: Car comes rolling up to scene of crime, siren blaring, lights flashing.*
- *Warning: "Halt, armed police officers!'*
- *Ultimatum: "Halt or we shoot!"*
- *Shoot.*

Choice (a) is the announcement level. You have to do this before you can do the others.

(b) 5 points: Provided it's phrased correctly, this could represent the warning level.

(c) 5 points: Yep, this kind of pressure always works well.

(d) 5 points: This is an ultimatum level action. It's easy to get five points here, because all of these are valid things to do. I guess I'm not saying that any of them is guaranteed to work, although I believe (c) would have the best chance of success. For a guarantee of success, you need to have a shoot level thing—for example, "no status report, no salary," or something like that. If you're starting to get to this level, you need to be checking your country's employment law.

Q.3

(a) 2 points: Okay, but I think you can do better this time.

(b) 5 points: Again, it's probably largely a question of style, but I think this is the way to go.

(c) 4 points: The "retrospective" bit will cheese them off, and may cause this to be not quite effective as (b). It'll still work, though.
(d) 0 points: It would want to be a particularly execrable training course for them not to pick up some useful ideas, but that is not the answer here.

Scores

13–15 points: Not too hard to get a high score here.

11–12 points: Maybe it's down to leadership style.

Less than 11: Maybe it's not!

Introduction

I've lost count of the number of organizations I've gone into that have some kind of quality certification such as ISO 9000 and whose project management is less then wonderful. This is equally true of places that are very highly proceduralized or that say "We use the blah methodology" or "We're a blah shop." Large companies are particular offenders in this regard.

Usually the problem is too many procedures or too much methodology. If you hear them utter the classic line "We generally use a subset of the methodology/the procedures," then that's your first indication that you may be in such a place.

My contention is that any procedure or methodology should implement the 10 steps. I would make four observations:

1. An almost mandatory first step in such a comparison is to create a glossary (i.e., to map the terminology used in your methodology/procedures to that used in the 10 steps).

2. If a particular procedural element is in the 10 steps and not in the methodology/procedures, then it's a gap in the methodology/procedures.

3. If a particular procedural element is in the methodology/procedures and not in the 10 steps, then unless it's either (1) very organization-specific or (2) a generally useful thing like a checklist, and then it's unnecessary.

4. There ought to be areas where your methodology/procedures and the 10 steps overlap.

In my experience, it's unusual to find anything in category (3). It's quite usual to find things in categories (2) and (4).

By doing such a comparison, it is possible to unearth places where your methodology/procedures have been letting you down and to tighten them. I think you'll agree this is a useful thing to do and very much in a spirit of continuous improvement, which should be part of any decent organization's agenda.

For completeness, you should do such a comparison in two stages. First, using your methodology/procedures as a baseline, analyze the 10 steps. Then do it the other way round just to make sure you haven't missed anything.

Comparing your methodology/procedures with the 10 steps

Here's what you do:

1. Start at the beginning of your methodology/procedures. For each procedural element determine whether it overlaps with the 10 steps (i.e., it is part of both your methodology/procedures and the 10 steps).

2. If not, is it very organization-specific? If yes, it goes in the "in ours but not in the 10 steps" bucket.

3. Is it a generally useful thing like a checklist? If yes, it goes in the "in ours but not in the 10 steps" bucket.

4. If it is neither very organization-specific nor a generally useful thing like a checklist, then it is an omission in your methodology/procedures.

5. Having completed this, now go start at the beginning of the 10 steps. For each element of the 10 steps, there should be an analog in your methodology. If not, then this is a gap in your methodology/procedures that needs addressing.

Adapting existing project management infrastructure/tools

If you do the analysis we have discussed in the previous section, you will end up with three bunches of things:

- Things you do that the 10 steps say you should do;

- Things you do that the 10 steps don't require;

- Things the 10 steps require that you don't do.

For those procedures/processes/tools that come into the first of these categories, no work is required. You should carry on doing these things. (Keep taking the tablets!) For those procedures/processes/tools that come into the second category, I would maintain that they are not necessary and can be jettisoned. For those items that come into the third category, you need to implement something that meets the particular requirement. Adapting something you already do—for example, replacing an existing status report template with one that is closer to the ones we've described in Chapter 2—may turn out to be a way to meet the requirement.

User assistance

A complete example of the comparison of a methodology with the 10 steps follows. As usual, the names have been changed to protect the innocent.

Structured Project Management (the 10 Steps) and the Acme Project Management Methodology

Contents

1 Introduction

This document provides a comparison between the Acme project management methodology (APMM) and structured project management, also known as "the 10 steps," described in *How To Run Successful Projects II—The Silver Bullet* (Prentice Hall, 1996).

It does so under four headings:

- Project terminology;
- Areas where the two approaches overlap;
- Areas in APMM but not in the 10 steps;
- Areas covered in the 10 steps but not APMM.

In the remainder of this document, a section is devoted to each of these headings. The reader's attention is also drawn to the introductory comments in Appendix 2 of *How To Run Successful Projects II—The Silver Bullet*.

2 Project terminology

The following table compares the terminology to be found in the description of APMM with the terminology of structured project management.

APMM Term	SPM Equivalent
• Advisory group	• Advisory group
• Activity	• Job
• Decision point	• Go/No-go decision
• Deliverable	• Deliverable
• Final report	• Project audit or postmortem
• Milestone	• Milestone
• Objective	• Goal
• Phase	• Phase
• Program management	• Program management
• Program manager	• Program manager
• Project	• Project
• Project managment	• Project management
• Project manager	• Project manager (or "trail boss")
• Project member	•Team member
• Project organization	• Project organization
• Project plan	• Project plan
• Progress report	• Status report
• Project schedule	• Project schedule
• Project specification	• Project specification (or "goal definition")

- Project sponsor
- Quality
- Stakeholders
- Steering group/project board
- Task

- Project sponsor (or "customer")
- Quality
- Stakeholders
- Steering group/project board
- Job

3 Areas where the two approaches overlap

This section describes areas where APMM and structured project management overlap.

3.1 The main phases of a project

Structured project management requires a project to be broken into phases, and the phases described in APMM satisfy this requirement. In addition, section 5 of the description of APMM provides a useful description of the jobs to be carried out in the various phases.

3.2 Planning the project

Step 1 of structured project management requires that the goal of a project be clearly defined and that its boundaries be fixed and not fuzzy. Section 5.2.2 of APMM identifies the importance of this by stating, "An important part of clarifying the task is to formulate its boundaries."

The remainder of Section 5.2.2 covers some of the same ground as structured project management's planning steps, steps 2–5. However, see some important omissions described below in Section 5.

3.3 Implementation of the project

Again this covers much of the same ground as structured project management's implementation steps, steps 6–10.

Again, however, there are some omissions described below in Section 5.

3.4 Project review

This is identical to the project audit in structured project management.

3.5 Project organization

Structured project management identifies four generic roles in a project:

- Customer;
- Management;
- Project manager;
- Team member.

These map easily onto the roles in APMM as listed in the following table.

APMM Role	Structured Project Management Equivalent
• Project sponsor*	• Customer
• Project sponsor	• Management
• Project manager**	• Project manager (or trail boss)
• Project members	• Team members
• User	• Customer or team member
• Recipient	• Customer or team member
• Monitor	• Team member
• Advisor	• Team member
• Suppliers	• Team members

*Possibly advised by steering group.

**Possibly advised by advisory group.

3.6 Project decisions

Structured project management requires a project to have phases, milestones, and decision points, and these requirements are satisfied in Section 7 of APMM. In addition, there is a large amount of useful guidance for the project manager as to how decisions are/should be made in the organization.

3.7 Project documentation

The four documents mentioned in Section 8 of APMM all have their analogs in structured project management, as listed in the following table.

APMM Document	Structured Project Management Equivalent
• Project specification	• Definition of the goal
• Project plan	• Project plan
• Progress report	• Status report
• Final report	• Project audit

3.8 Project tools

APMM identifies a number of possible support tools that can be used. The structured project management philosophy is to use the simplest tool possible that meets the particular requirement.

4 Areas in APMM but not in the 10 steps

Clearly the main difference between APMM and structured project management is that APMM is a specific company methodology while structured project management is a generic approach. Thus, there is an amount of useful detail in APMM that would be invaluable to a project manager running a project within the company. This is detail that could neither be known to, nor would it be appropriate in, an approach like structured project management.

5 Areas covered in the 10 steps but not APMM

The 10 steps cover a number of areas that are not covered in APMM. While the argument might be put forward that these are part of "good project management practice," our view is that these items are too important to be relegated to some form of professional training. Specifically, these are described in Sections 5.1–5.13.

5.1 Change control

While emphasizing the importance of fixing the boundaries of a project, APMM fails to emphasis sufficiently how all of this good work can be destroyed if subsequent changes to those boundaries are not controlled.

5.2 Importance of detail

APMM does not emphasize that an appropriate level of detail is the key to accurate project estimates, which in turn is one of the main elements of project success.

5.3 Role of the project manager

If the project manager is both manager and team member (i.e., has tasks to do on the project), APMM does not indicate which of these should take priority.

5.4 Suppliers as team members

APMM does not emphasize sufficiently that suppliers/subcontractors are also team members. "Our" parts of the project can be perfectly successful, but the project can still fail due to people over whom we have no direct control. This comment also applies to users and other project stakeholders.

5.5 Matching people to jobs

APMM says nothing about this crucial area.

5.6 Allowing for people's other commitments

Projects fail all the time because plans were based on resource availability that was never actually achieved. This is
not in any way highlighted in the sections of APMM to do
with planning the project.

5.7 Contingency

Contingency is *mandatory* in project plans. APMM fails to
mention this fact.

5.8 Dealing with "impossible missions"

Perhaps the biggest problem in project management is that,
for a whole variety of reasons, people commit to things that
are not humanly possible to do. (See earlier comments in
Section 5.2 about estimating.) APMM does not tell people
how to deal with this constant, real-world problem.

5.9 Leadership styles

Different leadership styles are right in different situations
and can greatly ease or add to the load on the project manager. APMM doesn't deal with this.

5.10 Progress reports

Structured project management differs from APMM in a
couple of areas here. Structured project management nor-
mally recommends weekly status reports unless the project is
very time-critical, in which case daily status reports would
be advised. Also, missing from the suggested progress report
contents is a fundamental piece of information—whether or
not the project is on target.

5.11 Daily/weekly routines

Structured project management provides daily and weekly routines to support the project manager in his or her day-to-day running of the project.

5.12 Historical project database

APMM falls short of recommending the establishment of a database of completed projects. This would, among other things, significantly improve the quality of future estimates.

5.13 Ten most common reasons why projects fail

There is a list available of the 10 most common reasons why projects fail and something like this might be useful input to Acme project managers, especially in the area of risk analysis.

In running a project, you give part of your "herd" to somebody else to trail-boss. Here's how to know whether or not that's a smart move — also, what to do if it turns out not to be.

11 Managing Subcontractors

Questions

Q.1 Your subcontractor has a good track record. However, on this project there's a definite lack of visibility of the final deliverables. There have also been a succession (i.e., at one stage five in a row) of missed status reports. What do you do?

(a) Ask the subcontractor if everything's okay and if it is, trust him or her to deliver, given his or her track record as a good and true magician.

(b) Wade in. Ask to see everything, if necessary poisoning the relationship in the process.

(c) Wait for more evidence.

(d) Stress again—this time in writing—the need for more visibility and that there must be no more missed status reports.

Q.2 The best way to start a subcontracted project out on the right foot is:

(a) Tell the subcontractor that your style is to micromanage everything.

(b) Convince the subcontractor you're a hard ass—your industry's answer to General George Patton.

(c) Ask the subcontractor to present its plan to a bunch of you for review.

(d) Convince the subcontractor you're a nice guy.

? Q.3 The best way to *run* a subcontracted project is:

(a) Micromanage everything.

(b) Be a hard ass.

(c) Be a nice guy.

(d) Get weekly non-day-at-the-beach status reports.

Answers

Q.1

(a) 0 points: And I don't believe this is "down to a matter of style." For you to take this course of action is basically for you to abdicate the complete success of your project to the subcontractor. If you're happy to do this, then you're a braver person than I.

(b) 5 points: I think it has to be. For me the five-in-a-row missed status reports is a dead giveaway. Whether he or she knows it or not, this subcontractor is in trouble.

(c) 0 points: How much "more evidence" do you need?

(d) 0 points: Yeah, yeah, yeah. I'll give you three points provided you do this as a prelude to (b). In other words, frame the memo such that the (almost inevitable) breach of it gives you the justification for action (b).

Q.2

(a) 0 points: Why? You won't be able to anyway.

(b) 0 points: Why? If subcontractors want to see Patton, let them get the movie out on video.

(c) 5 points: Yes. The correct answer, provided you do a thorough review as described earlier in Chapter 4 and that you follow through on any amendments to the plan that you ask the subcontractor to make. To put it more bluntly, don't allow the subcontracted piece of the project to start until you are 100% happy that the plan meets the criteria we have set down for a good plan. Perhaps an even better thing to do would be to make the quality of the plan one of the subcontractor selection criteria.

(d) 0 points: I'm sure you are! There now—you've convinced me!

Q.3

(a) 0 points: But only if you have evidence that the subcontractor is not doing the project management (trail-bossing) of the subcontracted bit. Then it's five points; otherwise it's zero.

(b) 0 points: Why bother? Unless that's the way God made you?
(c) 0 points: Can't hurt, but it's not the right answer.
(d) 5 points: Of course.

Scores

15 points: Everyone should have scored 15 here.

5–14 points: Because the questions weren't difficult.

0–4 points: Nor were they a matter of opinion. The issues were all about "evidence."

Introduction

Perhaps you remember the trail boss and cattle drive analogy from Chapter 1. In the situation where you decide to subcontract all or part of a project, you essentially decide to hand over the trail-bossing of part of your herd to somebody else. Rather than you taking the entire herd from the Rio Grande to Abilene, you decide to let another trail boss take a piece of your herd. Here we talk about the issues that arise in these circumstances. As you might have expected, we do so in two sections, one to do with the planning and the other with the execution of the plan.

Planning

I hope you'll forgive me if you feel that the opening part of this section belabors the point a bit. In my experience, while the logic involved in what follows would hardly tax the brain of a flea, these very obvious points that I'm making get missed in the general rush to get started and the wild optimism of the early part of the chase.

In deciding to give part of your "herd" of jobs to somebody else, the first point to remember is that herd is still your responsibility. We could never imagine John Wayne or Clint Eastwood riding into town at the end of our movie, with only a part of the herd, and blaming the other trail boss for the bit that got lost out on the prairies. In a subcontracting situation, the parts of the herd may make the journey to the eventual destination by different routes, but if you are the ultimate trail boss, then all of the herd (i.e., all of the jobs or the entire project) remains your responsibility.

It was Julius Caesar who said "fere libenter homines id quod volunt credunt," or "men usually willingly believe what they wish." Nowhere is this more true than in subcontracting. Sometimes, the statement "they are contractually bound to deliver X on time" becomes the same as "they *will* deliver X on time." These two things are not the same—except perhaps in the mind of some stressed-out project manager.

The next point to be made is that if somebody is going to act as a subcontractor, then either implicitly or explicitly that person is stating that he or she is taking responsibility for that piece of the herd. In other words, a subcontractor is going to provide project management for that piece of your project.

In my opinion, this is the key to your relationship with them from that point onward. All of the things you can validly either ask subcontractors to do or expect of them, the level of performance you are entitled to expect, how much or how little you interfere—all of these things—now become very clear once this connection is made.

Choosing the subcontractor

In choosing a subcontractor, it appears to me that what you want is somebody who will give the subcontracted piece of the project the same level of tender loving care that you are planning to give the rest of it. What's the key to this? A decent plan, of course. Thus, if you haven't yet chosen the subcontractor, give the candidates the brief and have them go away, build a plan, come back, and present it to you. Using the ideas we have discussed in Chapter 4, you can assess the presentations and decide which is the best plan.

The big issue in subcontracting, the issue that everyone seems to pussyfoot around is described as follows:

- If you're the subcontractor: How much should I let the client see into the internals of how I do my business?

- If you're the client: How much am I entitled to stick my nose into the subcontractor's business?

My view on this is very clear. At the plan presentation stage, you as client, are entitled to ask anything, no matter how detailed or trivial it may seem, to understand how the plan was formulated.

Details of how estimates were reached, whether the plans are based on eight-hour days, whether the plans have taken into account people's vacation days, how many people will be full-time and how many part-time, what are the skill levels of the people—these and a thousand other teeny-weeny details of the plan are yours, should you ask for them.

My experience has been that, in general, subcontractor plans fall well short of the standard we have set in Chapter 4. If this turns out to be the case, you are perfectly within your rights to send them back to the drawing board, having administered a sharp cuff around the ear!

Obviously, the quality of the plan isn't going to be the only selection criterion. However, the amount of time and effort it takes you to get an acceptable plan from your subcontractor can give you a useful first feeling for what the subcontractor is going to be like to work with. Equally, if some or all of them fail to see what you're driving at when you ask for the things that Chapter 4 requires, then you should perhaps count your lucky stars that you found out now and not when you were crossing a swollen river in a sandstorm while under attack from rustlers (if I may be permitted to lapse back into our movie, for a minute).

Writing the contract

Apart from the plan, your other big stick to beat the subcontractor with, at this stage, is the contract. You should build a contract based around the following if you are expecting them:

- Project deliverables at certain times;

- Status reports containing certain specific information at certain regular intervals.

Nobody's saying that you have to become an amateur lawyer to do this. In fact, in my experience, there are very few things more dangerous than such an amateur. However, given that the subcontracted piece of the project is going to become, to some extent, invisible to you, your picture of how it is unfolding can only be determined by the two sets of items listed above—project deliverables and project status reports. These then, are the items that you—with the help of your legal adviser—must ensure are built into the contract.

In addition, in the interests of prudent risk management, it's worthwhile specifying in the contract what you will do if some of these things fail to materialize. The plan is your best reference for doing this and ensuring that you cover all the bases. Work through the plan from left to right. Establish where the various input/responses from the subcontractor are expected. Now for each input/response, ask what will happen if that particular thing *doesn't* happen. Make it clear to the subcontractor that if things they were meant to do don't happen, then *they* are to blame—they are not providing the subcontracting service they are being paid to provide. The additional cost to you of doing *their* work gives you a guideline as to what fair penalties are.

So the negotiation might go something like this: If they fail to provide status reports to you, then—in the absence of this visibility, and for your own safety—you must audit the subcontractor's entire piece of the project. It's only fair that subcontractors should pay for this. If they object that by doing this you would be gaining knowledge of their proprietary tools or techniques, then your answer is—essentially—"tough!" That's the price they have to pay for not doing what they committed to doing.

Clearly, this is a great way of "debugging" a subcontractor's plan. You're essentially asking them to put their money where their mouth is, and you can pitch it to them as if you're helping them out. With a small amount of tact on your part, and given that you're at what Chuck Howell calls "the point of maximum goodwill and enthusiasm (i.e., the start of the project)," it should be possible to arrive at an agreement that the legals can then write in that language which only they know and love.

Of course, the subcontractor will be trying to play the same game with you. What if requirements or equipment that you were required to deliver don't show up? In these circumstances, be sure to build plenty of contingency into your activities so that you don't get stung.

At this point then, you have established a credible plan, and expectations have been set on both sides. You are now entitled to have these expectations met. Provided they are, then the project can remain a black box to you until the herd (hopefully) all shows up in Abilene one day? And if not, then the individual violations and the appropriate actions have been identified upfront in the contract.

Execution of the plan

The big issue in subcontracting—how much should I let the client see my business/how much am I entitled to stick my nose in—pops up again here. Basically, the deal is equally clear-cut. If the subcontractor does what they've committed to do, then you're required to keep your nose out of their affairs. If they don't, then you're not just entitled, but required, to wade in.

As we've seen, your contractual right in subcontracted situations are project deliverables and (ideally, weekly) non-day-at-the-beach status reports. If what you get is not the kind of status report that we've (I hope, by now) come to expect, or—worse still—if no status report appears, then this is evidence that something is amiss. *Evidence* is the key word here. Forget about bad or good feelings about a particular project, or subcontractor, or individual. Evidence is what it's all about. If the evidence is that the predicted progress is being made against the plan, then leave well enough alone. This is what you want, what you're paying for, and something you don't have the time to do yourself. This is the subcontracting relationship working as it should work.

Now, suppose things aren't quite so rosy. Status reports are either missed or are full of a worsening picture. Deliverables aren't appearing, but plenty of excuses are. One of these incidents by itself doesn't complete the picture, but a succession of them—with the evidence duly recorded by you—does give you a fair amount to go on. If at this point, you are unhappy with the way things are unfolding, you are entitled to wade in and ask to see everything and the kitchen sink.

What entitles you to do this? First, it's the contract. However, in the unlikely event that you had no contract at all, then quite simply, it's the fact that the whole herd still remains your responsibility. You're the one who's going to have to carry the can for it if it all goes wrong. So, if you're unhappy with the way you think it is going, and you can point to evidence that supports your view, then you have to wade in and sort it out.

In wading in and sorting it out, what do you actually do? Well, we're basically back to Chapter 5—assessing projects—and Chapter 6—rescuing projects—if it's gone that bad. Is it fair that you should have to do this, especially when they're being paid handsomely to do this work themselves?

No—it's not fair, but how many times has that word appeared in this book? It ain't fair but it comes with the territory; it's what you have to do if you're the trail boss.

If in doubt, go to your local video store and see if they can unearth a copy of Howard Hawks' *Red River* (1955) [8]. That will put you right on the roles and responsibilities of the project manager!

PART TWO

Implementing Structured Project Management in Organizations (iSPMiO)

In Part Two, the book introduces two new tools:

- The organization-wide status report (OSR) (Chapter 12);

- The project management performance model (Chapter 13).

Using these and the tools of Part One, the book shows—in Chapters 12 and 13—how it is possible to do the following:

- Understand where your organization is currently situated on the project management performance model (Chapter 14);

- Improve your organization's performance by moving it up the levels of the model (Chapter 15).

Chapter 16 illustrates these concepts with a pair of case studies. Then, Chapter 17 discusses how managers might organize their week to make maximum use of these ideas. Finally, Chapter 18 shows how all of the preceding ideas can be brought to bear on improving project management within an organization.

In this chapter, we introduce the first of two additional tools you will need to run your organization using structured project management.

12 The Organization-Wide Status Report (OSR)

Questions

? Q.1 The strategic objectives of your organization and the day-to-day operations are completely aligned with one another. How true is this statement for your organization?

(a) Not at all.

(b) Somewhat.

(c) Nearly.

(d) Completely.

? Q.2 Your goals for this year are so clear that everybody will know when they have been achieved. How true is this statement?

(a) Not at all.

(b) Somewhat.

(c) Nearly.

(d) Completely.

? Q.3 In your organization, everyone knows the big picture and his or her part in it. How true is this one?

(a) Not at all.

(b) Somewhat.

(c) Nearly.

(d) Completely.

Answers

Q.1
(a) 0 points: Not a good way to be, I think you'll agree.
(b) 1 point: Well, it's better than (a).
(c) 4 points: You have my admiration.
(d) 5 points: That's the way you want it.

Q.2
(a) 0 points: Tut, tut.
(b) 1 point: Maybe it's good to have them fuzzy. Then nobody will be able to assess your performance!
(c) 4 points: Good job.
(d) 5 points: Go on, go for the hat trick!

Q.3
(a) 0 points: I'm glad I'm not you.
(b) 1 point: Gonna be a tough year, huh?
(c) 4 points: Your modesty is one of your nicest features.
(d) 5 points: Can't be improved on.

Scores

15 points: Quite frankly, I wouldn't believe this.

12–14 points: You get my vote.

Less than 12: Let's change the subject—what do you do in your spare time?

Introduction

One of your first concerns if you run an organization is—or should be—what the status of the various projects under your direction is. The OSR provides you with a convenient way of seeing this at a glance.

What is an OSR?

Picture for a moment the following document. It has a front page. Listed on it, one line per project, are all of an organization's projects. It is the organization described as the sum of its projects.

The page has been printed on a color printer. The reason for this is that the page uses four colors—blue, red, orange, and green. Each line item is highlighted in one of these colors. They have the following significance:

- Blue: A plan has yet to be put in place for this project.

- Red: There are major problems with this project. It is off-target and has not achieved key milestones. Maybe corrective action has been taken, but whether it has or not, no improvement has been identified. There are significant project management issues that have not been resolved. The organization's senior management needs to be actively involved in this project, and decisions are required to recover it.

- Orange: Project may be off-target or may be having difficulty in achieving some of its key milestones. However, corrective action is being taken. There may be some project management issues. However, these are being addressed by the project manager, his or her manager, and the project's customer, if necessary. The organization's senior management should be kept up-to-date with progress/slippage and should be asked for their input/action when necessary.

- Green: Project is proceeding to target and is achieving key milestones. There are no project management issues or difficulties. No action is required by the organization's senior management.

That is the cover page. Attached to it then are a series of non-day-at-the-beach status reports, one per line item, for each of the projects identified on the cover page. This document is the OSR. It is published, certainly monthly, ideally weekly. If the leader of the organization is using it to steer the company, then the week-by-week changes to the OSR represent crucial information upon which decisions can/must be made.

Table B (in the color section of this book) presents an example of an OSR cover page with the names changed to protect the innocent; the example is from a small- to medium-sized company.

What use is an OSR?

Notice—and this is really important, so pay attention—that in the thinking behind, and construction of an OSR, we use the 10 steps of structured project management. What we are doing, quite simply, is treating our organization as a project. Let's look at this more closely.

Step 1   Visualize the goal.

An all-green OSR cover page is the goal we are heading toward when we begin applying structured project management to our organization.

Step 2   Make a list of jobs.

The OSR cover page shows the first-level breakdown of the jobs that go to make up the organization. As we put it earlier, it is the organization expressed as the sum of its projects.

Notice also, that the list of projects can be broken down to any level we like. (This is pure structured project management.) In the previous example, the project "sales in current territories" could break down into a series of projects, such as the following:

- Telesales;

- Major account 1;

- Major account 2;

- New sales campaign.

The sales department then might have its own OSR—cover page plus status reports—showing *its* projects.

If you have more than 25—the number was chosen arbitrarily—projects, you can always extend the OSR. However, a more sensible thing to do might be to put some structure on your list of projects so that at any level there are no more than 25 projects. The choice is yours.

Step 3 **There must be one leader.**
The OSR cover page and status reports both make it completely clear and unambiguous as to who is responsible for what.

Step 4 **Assign people to jobs.**
Again, this is completely clear from the OSR. Optionally, you can add fifth and sixth columns to the OSR cover page to indicate the following structured project management items:

- People-to-job classifications;

- Their trust/don't trust ratings.

Table C (in the color section of this book) presents the information provided in Table B with people-to-job classifications inserted.

A table like Table C enables the person running the organization to see at a glance where the problems are likely to be. (At the risk of stating the obvious, this might not be one you would want to leave lying around or posted up on notice boards!) You could also add columns for the following:

- Delivery date;

- Total project effort;

- A calculation of the project's PSI;

- Other key indicators that are important to you.

The important thing is not to put in too much clutter since this would obscure the original intent of the OSR, which is at-a-glance status reporting.

Step 5 **Manage expectations/have a margin for error.**
By regularly displaying OSR cover pages publicly and by regularly sending OSRs out to your management, to your peers, and to project teams (you might send slightly different versions), expectations are managed completely. Margins for error are maintained in individual projects through the use of contingency as we described previously.

Step 6   Use an appropriate leadership style.

As we already illustrated in step 4, you can record person-to-job classifications and trust/don't trust categorization on the OSR cover page, thereby reminding you of the right style to use with individual project managers.

Step 7   Know what's going on.

The OSR cover page enables you to see at a glance the health of your organization's projects. (You don't have to be able to read and you can still know!) The health of individual projects is dealt with in individual status reports.

Step 8   Tell people what's going on.

This is one of the fundamental purposes of the OSR, especially the cover page. It depicts graphically the state of the organization.

Step 9   Repeat steps (1) through (8) until (10).

You don't just do one OSR to take a snapshot in time. Operationally, as you run your organization, you have it front of you constantly. It drives your to-do list, your priorities, where you spend your time. On a regular basis, snapshots are released to the rest of the organization. Another advantage of the kind of status roll-up shown in OSRs is that it encourages honesty and accuracy in estimating status.

Step 10   The prize.

It's that all-green OSR cover page we mentioned at the beginning!

How good or bad is your project management? Here's a scale on which to place yourself—the second of the additional tools you'll need.

13

Project Management Performance Model

Questions

? Q.1 A written plan exists for your organization. It shows the tasks that have to be done. The effort involved in carrying out the tasks and achieving the goal has been quantified in some way. How true is this statement for your organization?

(a) Not at all.

(b) Somewhat.

(c) Nearly.

(d) Completely.

? Q.2 How do you know that the people who report to you can be relied on to make their piece of the plan happen?

(a) Because they can show you a plausible plan.

(b) Because you trust them.

(c) Because they have a track record.

(d) Because they said they would.

165

? Q.3 Take any of the people who report to you. How much would you bet that this person will make his or her piece of the plan happen?

(a) Pass—I can think of plenty of other ways to blow my money.

(b) $5.

(c) $20.

(d) $100 or more.

Answers

Q.1

(a) 0 points: So, how do you know if you have enough people? How have you been able to make commitments, etc.?
(b) 1 point: And do you have any plans to improve upon this somewhat?
(c) 4 points: That's my boy/girl.
(d) 5 points: A real goody two shoes, aren't you? I think I wouldn't actually believe this. How about you take four points?

Q.2

(a) 5 points: Plausible *is the key word here. You would score 0 without it.*
(b) 1 point: Really? (Said in a sarcastic rather than an inquiring tone.)
(c) 3 points: Yes, but the game we're playing this year isn't the game we've played last year or the year before.
(d) 0 points: Next time you go to buy a used car, take somebody with you.

Q.3

(a) 0 points: Interesting question, isn't it?
(b) 3 points: The fact that you're prepared to bet at all says a lot. What does the fact that you didn't choose (c) or (d) tell you?
(c) 4 points: Sounds like a good person.
(d) 5 points: Hire a few more like this, and you'll be able to get in a whole lot more golf.

Scores

13–15 points: There must be parts of your organization that really hum.

7–12 points: I think it's good to maintain a healthy insecurity.

Less than 7: On the other hand, you could go for unhealthy insecurity, like this.

Introduction

A question we are often asked when on consulting or training assignments is, "You must think we're terrible. How bad are we?" I have to say that, in my experience, it is those organizations that ask such questions that are generally the better ones. It is the ones that *don't* have this insecurity that I worry about.

Still, it's a valid question. Where does project management, as it is practiced in our organization, fit in with regard to our peers or to comparable organizations? If we build an OSR, and it is a kaleidoscope of colors, what does that tell us? Should we give up now or is there some hope for us? Furthermore, if there is hope, what should we do next?

There seem to be at least two schools of thought with regard to improving project management within the organization. They are the following:

- The ISO 9000/quality/performance model school. Make the project management processes better and the performance on projects will improve as a result. This is, far and away, the more popular one. ISO 9000 is a good example of this. So too is the Software Engineering Institute's capability maturity model (CMM) [9]. The basic thesis of the CMM, as expounded by its creator, Watts Humphrey, is that "the quality of a software system is governed by the quality of the process used to develop and evolve it."

- Hire project managers who have been certified by somebody like the Association of Project Managers (APM) or Project Management Institute (PMI). These people will carry out a recognizable, standard process to make projects successful.

We have taken a different approach here. In doing so, we fly in the face of a lot of conventional wisdom. As a result, I guess the first thing I have to do is explain why we have taken this approach. There are two reasons:

1. First of all, if we had to choose, if we could only focus on one thing, what would it be? The processes? The project managers? I don't think so. If we could focus on only *one* thing, it

would have to be the projects—*not* the processes or project managers, worthy as these are. Why? Well, because the projects are what our business is all about. If we don't do our projects, our business dies. Why then, if we want to improve our project management, should we not also focus on the projects? Let's try to get these right and, in getting them right, let's identify any process or project manager-related issues that stop us from doing that.

2. Second, much as we would like it to be, project management is not a production line process. The projects—especially these days—are too diverse. The people-related issues are too many, too complicated, ever-changing. What I'm really saying is that project management quality is variable; it's dynamic. It changes with the projects and the people. It may be good one year, bad the next. The fact that it was very good in one quarter doesn't guarantee it will be good for the next quarter—at least, not without plenty of vigilance. If we achieve a certain level of project management quality, there is no guarantee, in my opinion or my experience, that we can hold that level. "Hold the gains" was a motto I saw in somebody's office. Nowhere is this more true than in project management.

What we propose, therefore, is a model consisting of a scale and a pointer. The pointer can move up or down the scale. The organization should be constantly trying to move the pointer up the scale and hold the gains by not letting it slip back down again. If the pointer stalls within one of the five levels on the scale, then the organization will essentially do its project management as described in that level. To do so in level 1, for example, would be calamitous. To do so in level 5 would be wonderful. We present the scale and the pointer in turn.

Project management performance scale

It had been my original intention to call Table 13.1 a project management maturity model. Based on what I have just said, I now believe it is more accurate to call it a project management

Table 13.1   Project Management Performance Scale

Measurement categories	Level 1: Chaos	Level 2: The Dawn of Civilization	Level 3: Renaissance	Level 4: The Age of Enlightenment	Level 5: Nirvana
Management understanding and attitude	No comprehension of project management as a useful tool; tendency to blame project managers for project management problems	Recognizing that project management may be of value but not willing to provide money or time to make it all happen; saying that there is management commitment but management actions don't bear this out	Learning more about project management; becoming supportive and helpful	Participating; understanding absolutes of project management; recognizing their personal role in continuing emphasis	Consider project management as an essential part of the company system
Project management status	Project management is hidden in the various operational departments	Some initial training in project management, but the main emphasis is still on doing the day-to-day business; project management remains hidden in the operational departments	Project management is recognized as a key differentiator within the company	Best practice project management is used routinely within the company; every new endeavor structured as a project	The company is run as a series of hierarchical projects, the sum of the projects adding up to the company's strategic plan
Problem handling	Problems are fought as they occur; fire-fighting; no resolution; inadequate definition; lots of yelling and accusations	Teams or task forces are set up to tackle major immediate problems; long-term solutions are not sought	Concept of solving problems early becomes established within the company	Problems are identified early; everybody has a say in suggesting improvements	Except in the most unusual cases, problems are prevented
Project management improvement actions	No organized activities; no understanding of such activities	Trying short-term (motivational) fixes such as training; obvious "motivational" short-range efforts	Implementation of a project management improvement program (e.g., implementing structured project management across the organization)	Continuing the project management improvement program	Project management improvement is a normal and continued activity

Table 13.1   (continued)

Measurement categories	Level 1: Chaos	Level 2: The Dawn of Civilization	Level 3: Renaissance	Level 4: The Age of Enlightenment	Level 5: Nirvana
Summary of company project management position	"We don't know why we have project management problems"	"Do we really always have to have project management problems?"	"Through management commitment and project management improvement, we are identifying and resolving our problems"	"Project management improvement is a routine part of our operation"	"We know why we don't have project management problems"

performance scale. The entries in Table 13.1—I hope—are self-explanatory.

Let's look at the different levels of the scale represented in Table 13.1.

- *Level 1 (chaos)*. An organization at this level really has problems. In such organizations, fire-fighting is the norm, people work appalling hours, and management is viewed as part of the problem. There is often antagonism between management and the troops. If an organization in this state were to draw up an OSR it would almost certainly be a mixture of blues (predominant), reds (almost all of the rest), and the occasional orange. Greens, when they occurred, would occur because the magicians in those organization moved heaven and earth to get something done. It is probable that such an organization couldn't actually draw up a (truthful) OSR, because it simply doesn't have even the most basic infrastructure or information to enable it to do so. In good times, such an organization will oscillate but can survive depending on what kind of business it's in. In bad times, the oscillations could well be enough to make it crash and burn.

- *Level 2 (the dawn of civilization)*. This is the "there has to be a better way" organization. The organization that might be asking the question I cited above—"How bad are we?"—would most likely show up here. Typically, such an organization starts off sending some of its project managers on project management training courses as a first tentative step. An organization at this level will show some greens, but plenty of oranges, reds, and blues. This is a kaleidoscope organization. The OSR cover sheet shown in Table B (in the color section of this book) is for such an organization. Organizations at this level—if they are motivated to improve—will almost certainly be so because they will be experiencing some or all of the following symptoms:

  · Lack of clear direction and lack of focus. The organization is advancing on too many fronts. Loops are not being closed. There is a lack of follow-through or of thinking things through. There are plenty of (unpleasant) surprises.

- People missing an understanding of the big picture and their part in it.

- Not so much antagonism between management and the troops, but a feeling that what management says and what it does aren't necessarily the same thing.

- Lack of understanding of the organization itself—who is responsible for what—coupled with poor internal communication or too many (or not enough of the right kind of) meetings.

- Quality of customer service suffering or, if not suffering, certainly coming under pressure.

- Gaps in adherence to existing procedures.

- Questionable decisions and mistakes being made.

- Waste of effort, resources, and money.

- Financial loss.

- A feeling that people are at the limit, that they have no more "bandwidth," that they are trying to do too much with too little.

  If such an organization fails to do something about its problems it will do one of the following:

- Fail to realize its full potential;

- Shrink to a shell of its former self;

- Implode.

In bad times it will almost certainly do one of the latter two.

- *Level 3 (renaissance).* An organization at this level has removed its reds and blues. Any runaways (reds) have been stopped and turned around and all projects are working according to plans. Immediate improvements will be noticed in terms of the symptoms described above.

  - There is now clear direction toward a specific goal and very much improved focus. Things are thought through and followed through. The number of surprises has reduced. The ball isn't dropped as often as it used to be.

  - There is a feeling of management and troops pulling together.

Table A Organization-Wide Project Assignment for the ACME Corporation

ACME CORPORATION—ORGANIZATION-WIDE PROJECT ASSIGNMENT
DEMAND—EFFORT REQUIRED

Project	Who	Jan	Feb	Mar	Apr	May	Jun	Jul	Aug	Sep	Oct	Nov	Dec	Notes
Department management	JG	1	1	1	1	1	1	1	1	1	1	1	1	
Largo 3.3 & 4.1	AR	1	1	1	1	1	1	1	1	1	1	1	1	900 MD
	DH	1	1	1	1	1	1	1	1	1	1	1		
	JF	1	1	1	1	1	1	1	1	1	1	1		
	POC	1	1	1	1	1	1	1	1	1	1	1		
	MC		0.2	0.2	0.2	0.2	0.2	0.2	0.2					
Relish 3.5.09 & 3.6	CN		1	1			1	1						2 people for 2 months
	NB		1	1			1	1						
Bronze 4.0 & 5.0	JD		1	1	1	1				1	1	1		2 full time for 3 months; 2 part-time 3 months
	AR		1	1	1					1	1	1		
	RSV		0.4	0.4	0.4					0.4	0.4	0.4		
	JG		0.4	0.4	0.4					0.4	0.4	0.4		
EMU	JP	1	1	1	1	1	1	1	1	1	1	1	1	140 MM
	MG	1	1	1	1	1	1	1	1	1	1	1	1	
	TD	0.4	0.4	0.4	0.4	0.4	0.4	0.4	0.4	0.4	0.4	0.4	0.4	
	MW	1	1	1	1	1	1	1	1	1	1	1		
	JM	1	1	1	1	1	1	1	1	1	1	1		
	RG	1	1	1	1	1	1	1	1	1	1	1		
	ACC1						1	1	1	1	1			
	ACC2		1	1	1	1	1	1	1					
	ACC3		1	1	1	1	1	1	1					
	ACC4		1	1	1	1	1	1	1					
	RPG1				0.5	1	1	1	1					
	RPG2				0.5	1	1	1	1					
	RPG3		0.25	1	1	1	1	1	1					
	VISION		1	1	1	1	1	1	1	1	1	1		
	BC		0.5	1	1	1	1	1	1	1	1			
	DATA1							1	1	1				
	PK					0.5	0.5	0.5	0.5	0.5	0.5	0.5	0.5	
Y2K	JC		0.5	0.5	0.5	0.5	0.5	0.5	0.5	0.5	0.5	0.5	0.5	295 days
	AD		1	1	1	1	1	1	1	1	1	1	1	
	JDV		1	1	1	1	1	1	1	1	1	1	1	
	MC	0.2	0.2	0.2	0.2	0.2	0.2	0.2	0.2					
Reporting	POC	1	1	1	1									2.5 people × 3 months
	BC	1	1	1										
	CLSOL	0.5	0.5											
Modeling	CLSOL		0.5	1	1									4 months; 1 person
	JD		0.5	0.5	0.5									
DEFROST development	DELPHI		1											1
Lance development	DELPHI			1										1
SMOG development	Mr X		0.5	0.5										1
	SOC		0.5	0.5										
Accounts	PK		0.5	0.5	0.5									
Support	NOS	1	1	1	1	1	1	1	1	1	1	1	1	4 people full-time

Project DEMAND—EFFORT REQUIRED	Who	Jan	Feb	Mar	Apr	May	Jun	Jul	Aug	Sep	Oct	Nov	Dec	
Support	NOS	1	1	1	1	1	1	1	1	1	1	1	1	4 people full time
	SOC	0.5	0.5	0.5	0.5	0.5	0.5	0.5	0.5	0.5	0.5	0.5	0.5	
	PK	0.5	0.5	0.5	0.5	0.5	0.5	0.5	0.5	0.5	0.5	0.5	0.5	
	CN	1				1		1	1	1	1	1	1	
	Mr X		0.5	0.5	1	1	1	1	1	1	1	1	1	
	ANO1		1	1										
	ANO2		1	1	1	1	1	1	1	1	1	1	1	
Total person-months		16.1	33.3	34.6	30.1	27.8	28.8	29.8	28.8	31.2	24.2	22.2	19.4	326

SUPPLY SHORTFALL / OVERSUPPLY

WHO	Monthly availability	Month by month shortfall / oversupply											
		Jan	Feb	Mar	Apr	May	Jun	Jul	Aug	Sep	Oct	Nov	Dec
JG	1	0	0	0	0	0	0	0	0	0	0	0	0
AR	1	0	0	0	0	0	0	0	0	0	0	0	0
DH	1	0	0	0	0	0	0	0	0	0	0	0	0
JF	1	0	0	0	0	0	0	0	0	0	0	0	0
POC	1	–1	–1	–1	–1	0	0	0	0	0	0	0	0
MC	0.4	0.2	0	0	0	0	0	0	0	0.4	0.4	0.4	0.4
CN	1	0	0	0	1	0	0	0	0	0	0	0	0
NB	1	1	0	0	1	1	0	0	1	1	1	1	1
JD	1	1	0	0	0	0	1	1	1	0	0	0	1
AR	1	1	0	0	0	1	1	1	1	0	0	0	1
RSV	0.4	0.4	0	0	0	0.4	0.4	0.4	0.4	0	0	0	0.4
JG	0.4	0.4	0	0	0	0.4	0.4	0.4	0.4	0	0	0	0.4
JP	1	0	0	0	0	0	0	0	0	0	0	0	0
MG	1	0	0	0	0	0	0	0	0	0	0	0	0
TD	0.4	0	0	0	0	0	0	0	0	0	0	0	0
MW	1	0	0	0	0	0	0	0	0	0	0	0	0
JM	1	0	0	0	0	0	0	0	0	0	0	0	0
RG	1	0	0	0	0	0	0	0	0	0	0	0	0
ACC1 (Access #1)	1	1	1	1	1	1	0	0	0	0	0	1	1
ACC2 (Access #2)	1	1	0	0	0	0	0	0	0	0	1	1	1
ACC3 (Access #3)	1	1	0	0	0	0	0	0	0	0	1	1	1
ACC4 (Access #4)	1	1	0	0	0	0	0	0	0	0	1	1	1
RPG1	1	1	1	1	0.5	0	0	0	0	0	1	1	1
RPG2	1	1	1	1	0.5	0	0	0	0	0	1	1	1
RPG3	1	1	0.75	0	0	0	0	0	0	0	1	1	1
VB	1	1	0	0	0	0	0	0	0	0	0	0	0
BC	1	0	–0.5	–1	0	0	0	0	0	0	0	1	1
DATA1 (Dataease #1)	1	1	1	1	1	1	1	0	0	0	1	1	1
PK	1	0.5	0	0	0	0	0	0	0	0	0	0	0
JC	1	1	0.5	0.5	0.5	0.5	0.5	0.5	0.5	0.5	0.5	0.5	0.5
AD	1	1	0	0	0	0	0	0	0	0	0	0	0
JDV	1	1	0	0	0	0	0	0	0	0	0	0	0
CL	1	0.5	0	0	0	1	1	1	1	1	1	1	1
JD	1	1	0.5	0.5	0.5	1	1	1	1	1	1	1	1
DE	1	1	0	0	1	1	1	1	1	1	1	1	1
Mr X	1	1	0	0	0	0	0	0	0	0	0	0	0
SOC	1	0.5	1	1	1	0.5	0.5	0.5	0.5	0.5	0.5	0.5	0.5
NOS	1	0	0	0	0	0	0	0	0	0	0	0	0
ANO1	1	1	0	0	1	1	1	1	1	1	1	1	1
ANO2	1	1	0	0	0	0	0	0	0	0	0	0	0
Total oversupply/ shortfall	37.6	21.5	5.25	4	8	9.8	8.8	7.8	8.8	6.4	13.4	15.4	18.2

Table B OSR Cover Page Example

#	Project	Trail Boss	Status
1	Sales in current territories	Hoagy	Proceeding to plan
2	Marketing	Brian	Proceeding to plan
3	Admin.	Ben	Covered by ISO9002 procedures
4	Software	Steve	Beta availability 17 Nov
5	Reorganization	Steve	Proceeding to plan
6	Stock option scheme	Steve	Needs a plan
7	Current recruitment drive	Dave	Needs a plan
8	Cashflow	Erwin	Improvement plan in progress
9	UK operation	Dave	Needs a plan
10	Training	Charlie	Needs a plan
11	Long term investment	Steve	Needs a plan
12	People (HR)	Paddy	Needs a plan
13	Legal	Paula	Needs a plan
14	IT	Sam	Needs a plan
15	Apollo II	Dave	Needs a plan
16	USA	Dave	Needs a plan
17	Plan for next year	Dave	Needs a plan
18			
19			
20			
21			
22			
23			
24			
25			

Table C   OSR Cover Page with People-to-Job Classifications

#	Project	Trail Boss	Status	Category
1	Sales in current territories	Hoagy	Proceeding to plan	1
2	Marketing	Brian	Proceeding to plan	4
3	Admin.	Ben	Covered by ISO9002 procedures	1
4	Software	Steve	Beta availability 17 Nov	4
5	Reorganization	Steve	Proceeding to plan	1
6	Stock option scheme	Steve	Needs a plan	1
7	Current recruitment drive	Dave	Needs a plan	2
8	Cashflow	Erwin	Improvement plan in progress	4
9	UK operation	Dave	Needs a plan	4
10	Training	Charlie	Needs a plan	2
11	Long-term investment	Steve	Needs a plan	1
12	People (HR)	Paddy	Needs a plan	2
13	Legal	Paula	Needs a plan	4
14	IT	Sam	Needs a plan	2
15	Apollo II	Dave	Needs a plan	4
16	USA	Dave	Needs a plan	1
17	Plan for next year	Dave	Needs a plan	2
18				
19				
20				
21				
22				
23				
24				
25				

Table D   ETP Projects

#	Project	Trail Boss	Status	
1	Sales in current territories	FG	Proceeding to plan	1
2	Marketing	DF	Proceeding to plan	2
3	Admin.	WJ	Covered by ISO9002 procedures	1
4	Technology	WA	Beta availability 17 Nov 1997	1
5	Mgmt—restructuring	YN	Proceeding to plan	4
6	Mgmt—stock option scheme	WA	Needs a plan	1
7	People—current recruitment drive	YN (should be WJ)	Needs a plan	4
8	Finance—cashflow	WJ	Improvement plan in progress	1
9	Expansion into a new market	YN	Needs an audit and a rescue (plan to go forward)	4
10	Training & Consultancy—ongoing	YN	Needs a plan	2
11	Finance—long term investment	WA	Needs a plan	1
12	People—existing people	WJ	Needs a plan	1
13	Legal	WJ	Needs a plan	1
14	Technology—IT	SN	Needs a plan	4
15	Expansion	YN	Needs a plan	4
16	Expansion into a new sector	YN	Needs a plan	4
17	Mgmt—plan for 1998	YN	Needs a plan	1
18	Training & Consultancy— new product development	Unknown	Needs a plan	—
19				
20				
21				
22				
23				
24				
25				

Table E   OSI With Historical OPI

#	Name	Trail boss	1/22/99	1/29/99	2/8/99	2/15/99
	Sales and Marketing					
1	Sales forecasting	BI		0	0	
1.1	Garden court	BI	−1	0	3	
2	Actual sales	BI	0	0	0	
3	Marketing					
3.1	Competitive analysis	GG	3	5	5	
3.2	Telemarketing	ER	3	5	5	
3.3	Collateral	GG	3	5	5	
3.4	Web	GG	3	5	5	
3.5	Segmentation	GG	0	0	0	
4	SB—sales forecast	BI	−1	5	3	
5	SB—actual sales	BI	−1	5	−1	
6	SB—marketing	GG	−1	3	3	
7	Product management (inc. dev.)	Trail boss?	−1	−1	−1	
8	Commission scheme	BI	5	5	5	
9	Pricing	BI		5		
10	Filing	Trail boss?	0	0	0	
11	Financial reports	Trail boss?	0	0	0	
12	Database administration	BI		3	3	
13	Marketing research for subs.	BI	0	0	0	
	OPI =		0.6	2.1	1.7	
	Engineering					
1	1999 project plan	WA	3	0	5	
2	Training reqs	WA	3	0	5	
3	VAMP	YN	−1	3	3	
4	Knowledge management	BI	0	0	0	
5	Competitive analysis	GG	3	5	5	
6	Employee handbook	ER	3	5	5	
7	TCPM products	GO	0	0	0	
8	Case study	NN	3	5	5	
9	Product delivery syllabus	BE	0	0	0	
	OPI =		1.6	2.0	3.1	

#	Name	Trail boss	1/22/99	1/29/99	2/8/99	2/15/99
	PALFFF					
1	Personnel	RE	3	3	3	
2	Admin.	RE	5	5	5	
3	Legal	CO	5	5	5	
4	Facilities	RD	3	5	5	
5	Finance	PR	5	5	5	
6	Financial budget	BI	−1	5	5	
	OPI =		3.3	4.7	4.7	
	Information Systems	LL	−1	−1	−1	
	OPI =		−1.0	−1.0	−1.0	
	Manufacturing	DF	−1	0	1	
	OPI =		−1.0	0.0	1.0	
	PROJECT WESTWOOD	Trail boss?	0	0	0	
	OPI =		0.0	0.0	0.0	
	Overall OPI =		0.6	1.3	1.6	

Table F   Case Study #1 OSR

#	Project	Trail Boss	Status
1	Sales in current territories	Hoagy	Proceeding to plan
2	Marketing	Brian	Proceeding to plan
3	Admin.	Ben	Covered by ISO9002 procedures
4	Software	Steve	Beta availability 17 Nov
5	Reorganization	Steve	Proceeding to plan
6	Stock option scheme	Steve	Needs a plan
7	Current recruitment drive	Dave	Needs a plan
8	Cashflow	Erwin	Improvement plan in progress
9	UK subsidiary	Dave	Needs a plan
10	Training	Charlie	Needs a plan
11	Long term investment	Steve	Needs a plan
12	People (HR)	Paddy	Needs a plan
13	Legal	Paula	Needs a plan
14	IT	Sam	Needs a plan
15	Apollo II	Dave	Needs a plan
16	USA	Dave	Needs a plan
17	Plan for next year	Dave	Needs a plan
18			
19			
20			
21			
22			
23			
24			
25			

Table G   Case Study #1 OSR — One Month Later

#	Project	Trail Boss	Status
1	Sales in current territories	Hoagy	Proceeding to plan
2	Marketing	Brian	Proceeding to plan
3	Admin.	Ben	Covered by ISO9002 procedures
4	Software	Steve	Beta availability 17 Nov
5	Stock option scheme	Steve	Needs a plan
6	People—recruitment	Ben	1998 hiring plan in progress
7	Finance—cashflow	Ben	Improvement plan in progress
8	UK operation	Clint	Needs a plan to go forward
9	Delivery	Neil	Needs a plan
10	Long term financing	Fergus	Needs a plan
11	People—existing	Ben	Needs career development plans
12	Legal	Ben	Legal audit done and being implemented
13	IT	Steve	Needs a plan
14	Another subsidiary	Charlie	Send stuff to Charlie
15	Next generation product	Tony	Waiting on plan from Tony
16	Alliances	Natalie	Review agreement
17	Alpha project	Herman	Needs a plan
18	Beta project	Marjorie	Needs a plan
19	New software	Aurora	Needs a plan
20	Facilities	Ben	Needs a plan
21	Aardvark project	Fergus	Needs a plan
22			
23			
24			
25			

Table H   Case Study #1 OSR — Three-and-a-Half Months Later

#		Project	Trail Boss	Plan?	Status Reports?
1		ETP Group	Fergus	Plan is the sum of other plans plus 1.1 and 1.2	Yes
	1.1	Development capital	Fergus	Plan done	No
	1.2	Stock option scheme	Fergus	Plan being implemented	No
2		Ireland			
	2.1	Delivery	Neil	Neil is doing a plan	No
	2.2	Sales & Marketing	Hoagy	Plan being implemented. Need a marketing plan for 1998.	Yes
	2.3	People	Ben	1998 hiring plan in progress	Yes
	2.4	Admin.	Ben	Covered by ISO9002 procedures	Yes
	2.5	Legal	Ben	Plan being implemented	Yes
	2.6.1	Finance—cashflow	Ben	Plan being implemented	Yes
	2.6.2	Finance—budgets/ reporting	Tom	Needs a plan	No
	2.7	Facilities	Ben	Consider as part of investment	Yes
	2.8	IT	Steve	Need to present plan	No
	2.9	Next generation product	Tony	Tony doing a plan	No
	2.10	Derivative products	Udam	Has a plan	No
3		Software			No
	3.1	Current product	Steve	Plan done	No
	3.2	New product	Aurora	Consider as part of investment	No
4		UK operation	Clint	Plan in place	No
5		Another subsidiary	Charlie	Plan in place	No
6		Alpha project	Herman	Plan in place	No
7		Beta project	Marjorie	Plan in place pending Board approval	No
8		Alliances	Natalie	Consider as part of investment	No
9		Aardvark project	Fergus	Consider as part of investment	No

Table 1   Instrument Panel for Organization

	Jan	Feb	Mar	Apr	May	Jun	Jul	Aug	Sep	Oct	Nov	Dec
Project A	−1	−1										
Project B	−1	0										
Project C	−1	0										
Project D	5	5										
Project E	0	0										
Project F	−1	3										
Project G	−1	−1										
Project H	0	0										
OPI	0.0	1.0										
Step 1	4	10										
Step 2	4	10										
Step 3	4	5										
Step 4	3	5										
Step 5	0	0										
Step 6	15	30										
Step 7	4	4										
Step 8	4	4										
Step 9	4	4										
Step 10	0	0										
PSI	27	42										
Project A	4DT	4DT										
Project B	5	5										
Project C	4DT	4DT										
Project D	1T	1T										
Project E	2T	2T										
Project F	4DT	4T										
Project G	2T	2T										
Project H	4DT	4DT										

- It is clear to all in the organization how the structure of the organization has been engineered so as to focus on the clear direction and goal.
- The quality of customer service has improved.
- Gaps in adherence to existing procedures have been closed.
- There is a feeling that the organization is getting more "bang for the buck" both in terms of company dollars and people's time and energy.

    A comprehensive program of project management training, consulting, and mentoring is probably running during the transition from level 2 to level 3. Such an organization will have begun the building of a historical project database and will have experienced the significant improvements such a database brings with it.

- *Level 4 (the age of enlightenment).* The organization has achieved "all green" status on a day when it was able to report that all of its project were green. Sometimes, some of the organization's projects may drift back into orange, or (very rarely) into red. However, when this happens, a set of clearly defined procedures, based on structured project management, move automatically and easily into place. The organization has a comprehensive historical project database that is now central to all of its processes. The organization "hums" with a feeling of steady progress toward clearly defined goals, and milestones are being achieved. The project management program continues, but it is now completely organization-specific, and almost low-key. It has become part of the furniture.

- *Level 5 (nirvana).* An organization runs for longer and longer periods of time with nothing but green projects. Projects going orange are a rarity, due both to the power and sophistication of the historical project database and the commitment of all people in the organization to the principles of structured project management. This is a commitment that has not been brought about through sanction or edict from above, but through the clear benefits that all in the organization have gained from structured project management. When projects do go orange, they are seen as an opportunity to learn, to improve even further. The project management program has merged so much into the organization's culture that it has become indistinguishable from it.

Pointer — the organizational performance indicator (OPI)

The OPI is positioned on the scale by using the OSR—see Chapter 12—as its basis for calculation. Thus, the organization's project performance is distilled down to a single value, which gives us feedback on how the organization's projects as a whole are proceeding and where room for improvement lies.

The calculation is done as follows:

- For each green, score 5.

- For each orange, score 3.

- For each blue, score 0.

- For each red, score −1.

Add up all the scores and divide by the total number of projects. This is the OPI.

For example, using the OSR from Table B, we can make the following calculations:

- $5 \times green = 5 \times 5 = 25$;

- $3 \times orange = 5 \times 3 = 15$;

- $1 \times red = 1 \times -1 = -1$;

- $8 \times blue = 8 \times 0 = 0$.

Thus, the total score is 39, and the total number of projects is 17. Therefore, the OPI is 2.3, and there are nine projects at risk.

Taking the 2 in front of the decimal point, we say that this puts the organization in level 2. It's a "could do much better" level as witnessed by more than half the projects being either out of control (red—1) or without plans (blue—8).

In this chapter, we show you how to figure out the state of all your organization's projects.

14 Figuring Out Where You Are

Questions

Q.1 Your organization consists of you as leader, five direct reports, and a team of 30 people. How much time is this going to need from you in terms of management?

(a) All your time (i.e., it's a full-time job).

(b) Half your time.

(c) It's the work of three people.

(d) Dunno, but I seem to work harder every year.

Q.2 You run your own company. You started it several years ago; it's grown rapidly, and now, conscious of your own limitations, you feel the time has come to "strengthen your management team." What do you do?

(a) Enroll them all in the local gym.

(b) Hire a hotshot CEO.

(c) Figure out a management structure, use the rule of thumb from the answer to question 1 to calculate how much effort is needed where, write profiles for the various positions, and fill them from new or existing staff, focusing on trying to get the closest match to the profile.

(d) Enroll all of your current managers in MBA programs or other training.

❓ Q.3   You've just joined a new company, and the organization you're going to run definitely needs a new management structure. How do you do it—that is, how do you "figure out a management structure"?

(a) Buy the latest and greatest management bestseller—it'll tell you.

(b) Use a hierarchical structure, but a somewhat flat one—that is, not with too many layers.

(c) Use a matrix structure with dotted line reporting, where necessary.

(d) Make sure every piece of your organization has somebody responsible for it.

Answers

Q.1

(a) 0 points: You probably spend all your time there, but that's not the proper way to approach the question.

(b) 5 points: Provided—and this is a big "provided"—the five are doing their jobs, the calculation is this: You are managing five people. Over a year this represents a five-person-year project. Assuming 220 person-days per person-year, this is 1,100 person-days; 10% of this (see Chapter 1) gives 110 person-days. Spread over 220 elapsed days (i.e., a year) then this is half a day every day.

(c) 5 points: Yes. If none of the five are doing their jobs properly, then you're right. In that case, you end up managing 35 people. That's 7,700 person-days, and 10% of that is 770, which spread over 220 days is actually the work of three and a half people. (The answer assumed that your five managers did some bit of their job properly!)

(d) 0 points: I don't doubt it.

Q.2

(a) 2 points: Won't solve any of your management problems, but should prolong their life expectancy. (Actually, I just realized—maybe you don't want that, Mr. Machiavelli!)

(b) 1 point: Put the monkey on someone else's back? It's a well-worn management technique, but it doesn't necessarily fix the problem.
(c) 5 points: Of course.
(d) 2 points: Can't hurt, but it's a long-term measure. Depends—among other things—on what kind of hurry you're in.

Q.3
(a) 1 point: It might.
(b) 3 points: You could.
(c) 3 points: You could.
(d) 5 points: Hey—the old ones are best! (I'll expect a call from a management theorist within hours of publication.)

Scores

13–15 points: You did well to score this high here.

9–12 points: Scary questions, some of them, huh?

Less than 9: Really scary questions, huh?

Introduction

Using the OSR and performance model described in Chapters 12 and 13 it is now possible to get a handle on the state of our projects and, hence, the state of project management in our organization. We accomplish this by doing the following things:

1. Define the organization as the sum of its projects;

2. Produce an OSR by doing a "soft" audit;

3. Calculate the organization's OPI and identify its performance level.

Organization as the sum of its projects

As we have said, the first step is to describe the organization. We want to do so not in terms of its mission statement, or its balance sheet, or its strategic plan, or its business plan, or its organization chart, or its market segments, or any of the million-and-one other ways one can describe an organization. Rather, we want to do it in terms of its projects. Specifically, we want to define the organization to be the sum of its projects.

We do this first at the topmost level. As we have said earlier, we try to limit the number of projects at this first level to (an arbitrary) 25. Then what we can do is take each of those items—one of which might, for example, represent a large organization in its own right—and break it down further on subsequent OSR cover sheets. Beginning at the top of an organization and working downward, getting others to fill in their organizations, we can, at the end, get down to individual people and their jobs. This process is described as follows:

1. Start at the topmost level. What are the projects that make up the organization? Look at the organization chart, and this should give you a fair idea. If you were explaining the organization to somebody else, how would you draw it? What big blocks would you identify? These are your first-level projects. If you're puzzled, look in the User Assistance section of this chapter for a worked example.

2. Now go one level down. In other words, take one of the top-level projects and begin to break it down further. You should probably involve the person who runs that particular project (e.g., if the top level project you chose was marketing, now look inside that project, along with the head of marketing) and see what projects make it up.

3. You can stop as soon as you feel you have a reasonable view of things—certainly no more than three levels, I would say.

4. At each level your aim is to ensure that you capture *all* of the projects.

5. Somebody—maybe not you!—should get a kick out of those moments when somebody is heard to utter the immortal words, "Hey, I didn't know we were doing that."

Soft audit

A soft audit is the simplest thing in the world. It is completely nonthreatening to the person being audited and only takes a matter of minutes.

To do a soft audit of a project, you ask the project manager the following questions:

1.   Does the project have a plan? (You don't even ask to see it if he or she claims that it does.) If not, the project should be shaded blue on your OSR. Otherwise go to question (2).

2.   Is the project on target? If the project manager says yes, the project is shaded green on the OSR. (Basically, you take his or her word for it!) Otherwise go to question (3).

3.   If the project is not on target, how off target is it? If the project manager answers phrases like "a little bit," "not too bad," "we'll make up the ground we've lost" (sure!), then you again take his or her word for it and shade the project orange on the OSR. Otherwise, go to question (4).

4.   Confirm with the project manager that the project has gone ballistic and is out of control. If he or she confirms this, then shade the project red on the OSR. Otherwise take him or her back to question (3), and if you can't get a reading there, try questions (1) or (2).

5.   All projects *must* be given some rating and color code.

Calculate the OPI

Now do the arithmetic and come up with the OPI, as described in Chapter 13. Position the OPI on the performance scale and that gives you your first reading on the state of your organization and its projects.

User assistance

To show you how to do this, I will use our own company, ETP, as an example. This is not because it is either a good or a bad example, but for a number of other reasons:

1.   For a book like this, it is an example of manageable size.

2.   I know its details intimately and thus can share a lot of information that I might not either (1) have access to or (2) be able to divulge if another company were chosen as an example.

Also I will stay at one level—the uppermost one—with the implication always that anything we are doing at this level can be replicated at any and all levels below. This example is based on ETP as it was a couple of years ago. As always, the names have been changed to protect the innocent.

For the purposes of this example, ETP consists of the following 10 functional areas:

- Sales;

- Marketing;

- Administration (admin.);

- Human resources (preferably called "people");

- Finance;

- Legal;

- Training and consulting;

- Technology;

- Management (mgmt.);

- Expansion.

In November 1997, ETP consisted of 18 projects. The projects are shown on an OSR cover sheet, depicted in Table D (in the color section of this book). Each project is described briefly as follows, with an accompanying discussion of the reasons for the color coding.

1. *Sales in current territories:* Sales are currently on target here and so this project is coded green.

2. *Marketing:* We are engaged in a major overhaul and enhancement of all aspects of our marketing from products and product positioning through marketing methods to marketing materials. A detailed plan exists for this project, but there have been no status reports and obvious signs of progress are somewhat lacking. Hence it has been coded orange.

3. *Admin.:* ETP has ISO 9002 certification. The set of ISO 9002 procedures are richest in the admin. area. These procedures

are essentially the "plan" to which admin. runs. Corrective actions are generated when any hiccups occur, and procedures are updated where necessary. It would be true to say that admin. is rarely anything other than green.

4. *Technology:* The project has a plan and is running to target. Weekly status reports, which are non-day-at-the-beach are being produced. This is coded green.

5. *Mgmt.—restructuring:* The company is currently restructuring to prepare itself for the next phase of growth. Since all restructurings involve change—sometimes traumatic change—a carefully thought through sequence of events has been put in place. Restructurings can have unpredictable consequences and so a comprehensive backup plan is in place. This project is on target and is coded green.

6. *Mgmt.—stock option scheme:* The company is implementing a stock option scheme. This is one of those projects that was running smoothly, then got caught up in issues to do with investment and expansion and was becalmed for a while. Steps are now being taken to put it back on the rails. Since these have not yet been completed, and a plan is not fully in place, the project is coded orange.

7. *People—current recruitment drive:* We are currently engaged in significant expansion. A recent recruitment drive brought a response that exceeded our wildest expectations—good news, but the result is that we are having difficulty getting through the volume of applicants. This is coded orange because the plan to complete this is not yet clear. It would be true to say we are in fire-fighting mode on this, and we need to move to regular-and-steady-progress-against-the-plan mode.

8. *Finance—cash flow:* Expansion always puts a strain on cash flow. That's why it's coded orange!

9. *Expansion into a new market:* This is a project that has gone badly awry. The reason? It was started without a comprehensive plan, of course. It needs an audit to figure out why we are where we are and then a plan to take us from there to where we want to be. This is coded red.

10. *Training and consultancy—ongoing:* Our training and consultancy division needs someone to head it up. (Hence, the recruitment drive—you see, there is method in our madness!) Hence also the lack of a trail boss. The lack of a trail boss explains the lack of a plan. The lack of a plan explains why it is coded blue.

11. *Finance—long-term investment:* Long term, the strain on cash flow will be eased by attracting some long-term investment into the company. We have just made the decision to go down this road, and a plan needs to be put in place—hence, the blue.

12. *People—existing people:* This is the administration of the normal business of human resources—contracts, salaries, career development plans. As you would expect in a young and rapidly expanding company, a certain amount of structure needs to be put on this function, which up until now, would have been lacking or low on the priority list. It is coded blue to indicate that we need a plan to put this structure in place.

13. *Legal:* We are in the throes of completing an audit of all our legal requirements over the next few years. From this will flow a plan, but at the moment this is coded blue.

14. *Technology—IT:* This is about the IT infrastructure needed to support the company. Up until now we have been reacting to immediate needs. A plan showing short- and medium-term objectives needs to be put in place. It is coded blue.

15. *Expansion:* This covers the overall strategy for the expansion of ETP. An updated version of this needs to be produced. It is coded blue.

16. *Expansion into a new sector:* This needs to be planned. It is coded blue.

17. *Mgmt.—plan for 1998:* The detailed business plan for ETP for 1998 needs to be produced. It is coded blue.

18. *Training and consultancy—new product development:* ETP will launch a major new product offering in 1998. This all needs to be planned. It is coded blue.

As can be seen, the company has lots of challenges. It is trying to do an awful lot, and the amount of blue indicates there is much planning work to be done. Some of these blues have obvious deadlines (e.g., the plan for 1998), so we need to make sure we get these started in good time. The orange projects need to be looked at. The green ones can be left to themselves with a minimum of interference and just the normal standard checks of structured project management.

However, there is one thing that cannot wait. It is staring us in the face. The red project is in trouble. It is hemorrhaging money. This needs to be fixed. Sure some of the blues are urgent too, but if we could only do one thing—and this is what prioritizing is all about—then it has to be to fix the red one. We will turn to this shortly, but first we have to look at the other important aspect of each of these projects—who is each project's trail boss?

Structured project management says that every project has to have one and only one leader. This applies whether your organization is, say, like ETP—medium-sized and already very project-focused—or a large multinational with a fixed, hierarchical, line management structure. Identifying one leader in the latter situation may be more difficult, and the chain of command that person has to follow—up their line to their manager, across to that person's peer in another function, and then down the chain there—may be more cumbersome, but the principle remains unaltered.

One of the most obvious reasons for the principle—I hasten to add that it's by no means the only one—is that, without a trail boss, or someone to take ownership of the project, it is unlikely that the thing will get rolling at all. A plan is the first step in structured project management. Without a trail boss, it is unlikely if even that step will be taken, or if it is taken, taken correctly.

Looking back at the example above, we are in reasonable shape, though things aren't perfect. Project 7 needs to have a switch in trail bosses. Seven projects have one person's name on them, which perhaps raises the question of whether that person is overworked and whether they're actually being project managed at all. The final project still doesn't have a trail boss, and this needs to be fixed.

After Chapter 14, you know where you are. Here, you start to make it better.

15 Start Making It Better

Questions

? Q.1 Your organization is well established, as are its competitors. An unspoken sort of "truce" exists between you and your competitors—this year maybe you steal a percentage point or two of market share; next year it swings back toward one of them. Live and let live. Everybody's making a living, and while things may not always run to target, "the important things always get done." What should you do?

(a) Do nothing—if it ain't broke, don't fix it.

(b) Be very afraid—things won't always be like this.

(c) Quantify how many things "may not always run to target" and whether "the important things" do always get done.

(d) Calculate how many years to your earliest retirement date, and if it's a number less than five, do nothing.

? Q.2 Your organization is young, growing fast, in a high-technology area, and—to some extent—blazing a trail. Like any group of managers, those that report to you are of mixed ability, but this is compounded by the nature of your business. What's the best support you can give to your managers?

(a) Mentoring.

(b) Micromanagement.

(c) Stock options, bonuses, large salaries, big cars, or other performance-based financial incentives.

(d) Get rid of the poorer ones and try to hire in hotshots.

Q.3 Same scenario as the previous one. It's clear to you that the Internet and Web are going to be a key part of your company's strategy going forward. What's your next move?

(a) Identify your requirements—what you would be trying to achieve by using this technology.

(b) Bring in presentations from a number of companies who specialize in Web work.

(c) Bone up on the technology yourself.

(d) Go looking for Web design people or companies.

Answers

Q.1
(a) 0 points: Oh, I don't think so.
(b) 3 points: Do indeed be very afraid. However, fear isn't enough. That's why it's 3 points.
(c) 5 points: "If you can't measure it, you can't manage it," the old saw goes. A promising start.
(d) 0 points: You don't have that long.

Q.2
(a) 5 points: I think so. You want to strengthen them, but not end up doing their job for them.
(b) 2 points: This is doing their job for them. You may have to on occasions, but if you end up doing it all the time, then you'll end up massively overloaded.
(c) 1 point: Great if they have potential that can be nurtured (mentored). Forget it, if they don't.
(d) 2 points: Get rid of the poorer ones—certainly, you'll have to, because of answer (b). Hire in hotshots? The problem you'll run into there, I fear, is that you won't be able to find them because they just don't exist. I think the holistic answer to this question is probably a mixture of all these

things, your ultimate aim being to get all of them to a point where you are confident that they can do their jobs.

Q.3
(a) 5 points: (To be said in a slightly bored voice.) Yes—solid police work!—it's been true for thousands of years, and it remains true now. What's the goal? What are you trying to achieve? If you don't know what port you're sailing to, then any wind is a fair wind.
(b) 0 points: Leave the class.
(c) 0 points: Not your next move, it isn't.
(d) 0 points: Leave the class. Go on—get outside the door.

Scores

15 points: Good one.

7–14 points: It ain't easy, is it?

Less than 7: Okay, you can come back into class.

Introduction

You've figured out where you're starting from. Now how do you start making it better? And maybe an even more immediate question—where do you start? In this chapter, we fix the starting point and take you through the sequence of events that should ensue.

Fix the reds

Your first, absolute priority is to fix the reds. If there are a number of these, pick the largest or most organization-critical one. These are the projects that have gone wildly out of control. We sometimes call this process "reining in runaways."

To do this you use the techniques that we described in Chapter 6. The outputs from such an exercise will be the following:

- The issues that caused the project to go wrong in the first place;
- The revised plan that has been successfully sold to the powers that be.

The issues get fed into a process we will describe later in this chapter. The revised plan means that this project ceases to be a red and can be reset to green. You then move on to the next red one.

The day on which the last red disappears from the OSR cover sheet is a significant one for the organization. "No more reds day" is a cause for celebration. It marks a significant watershed in any organization. It is a point at which the organization has said "enough is enough" and recognized that there is indeed a better way. The amount of self-examination, work, commitment, shock, and cultural change involved in clearing these cannot be underestimated.

Clear the blues

Once you have taken care of all the reds, it's time to turn your attention to the blues.

Blues are projects without plans. To get rid of a blue, what is essentially needed is to allocate a trail boss and get him or her to scope the project and prepare a plan as described in Chapter 2. The outputs from such an exercise will be the following:

- A project with a plan;

- Issues within or outside the project that needed to be/still need to be resolved for the project to succeed.

Once again, the issues get fed into the process we will describe shortly. The project with a plan means that this project ceases to be a blue and can be reset to green. You then move on to the next blue one.

Blues may sometimes have to take precedence over reds because of particular set deadlines (e.g., a statutory date such as Y2K, or in Europe, the launch of the Euro). However, in general, I would advise that you think very carefully before putting effort into blues rather than reds. Reds are already hurting the organization. If they are floating around, then scarce resources are already being wasted on them. Far better to fix this waste than start new projects involving even more scarce resources.

It would probably make a good title for a song—a happy song—but "no more blues day" is your next cause for celebration. It means that (1) all existing projects are now running to plans, that (2) there are no more runaways, and that (3) any new projects that emerge are not allowed to see the light of day without a plan.

The facts that all its projects have been planned and that the birth of any new project is marked with a plan means an enormous injection of reality into the organization. At last we are cutting our cloth to suit our measure (if that's how the saying goes). For perhaps the first time ever, the following are completely aligned and in synch:

- What must be achieved;

- Our capability to achieve it.

By now your OSR cover sheet will be a mixture of greens, projects that are on target, and oranges, projects that have drifted off the straight and narrow. If you are at this stage, many of the latter will be due to the newness of everything you are doing and the fact that it does take a bit of time to get these things right. Also, your database of historical projects will still be evolving and this will be key to getting to all green.

When an organization reaches the point at which the following are true, it has made an extraordinary achievement:

- All projects are working to plans.

- There are no more runaways.

- All new projects are born with a plan.

Search and destroy oranges

A project can go orange at any time. Orange represents a surprise on the project. Once you have fixed the reds and cleared the blues, you need to begin a process that essentially amounts to "eternal vigilance."

An orange can be thought of as a baby red. Reds are an accumulation of oranges, oranges either not recognized or recognized and ignored. Given enough time and feeding, an orange will grow into a red. In searching and destroying oranges, you set out to try to stop that process. To quote Tom Gilb, "If you don't actively attack the risks, the risks will actively attack you." As soon as a project goes orange, you don't want to give it any time to mature. You want to kill it now and learn all that is to be learned from the fact that it happened.

If there are no more reds and blues, then your task is to continuously scan the oranges and greens. The oranges you want to make green as quickly as you can. The greens you want to stay green. It goes without saying—but I'll say it anyway—that the following are true:

1. Every time a new project appears, you make it blue and then set out to convert it to green as quickly as possible.

2. Should a project become red, it goes to the top of the priority list and must be dealt with as a matter of urgency.

How do you go about spotting an orange? There are a number of ways:

1. The status report for that project tells you that it is.

2. No status report appears. I have come to the conclusion— after many bad experiences—that the nonappearance of a status report counts as a significant piece of evidence that things are not well on the project.

3. You can run a hard audit on the project. To do this you would use the techniques we described in Chapter 5.

4. You could commence a program of spot checks, or random hard audits. The purpose of these would be to "sweep" for projects in trouble.

5. When all else fails, you may just have a hunch. In [1], I described a number of negative signs to be found on projects. Maybe you'll see one of these—or maybe you'll just wake some time in the middle of the night with a cold sweat down your spine. It could be too much coffee; on the other hand, it could be that project.

Once you have determined that you have an orange on your hands, you do the following:

• Understand what happened—the hard audit (Chapter 5) process will tell you;

• Fix it and return the project to green status.

The outputs from such an exercise are listed as follows:

- A project running to a plan;

- Issues within or outside the project that needed to be/still need to be resolved for the project to succeed.

Resolve issues

The three processes previously described will result in issues that need to be fixed. These issues will be of two types:

1. Within-project issues;

2. External-to-project issues.

(For issues to do with subcontractors or subcontracts, you can simply adopt a convention that either such issues are "within-project"—i.e., How is the project manager managing this subcontract?—or "external-to-project"—because it *is* a subcontract.) Both types must be dealt with.

Within-project issues

I would be prepared to stake quite a large amount of money that any within-project issues that occur will be drawn from the list we first presented in Chapter 1—the 10 most common reasons why projects fail. These reasons are listed again as follows:

1. The goal of the project isn't defined properly (i.e., the goal isn't bounded, or all of the stakeholders are identified, or stakeholders' win conditions aren't identified).

2. The goal of the project is defined properly, but then changes to it aren't controlled (i.e., there is no effective change control).

3. The project isn't planned properly (i.e., it is not planned in accordance with the principles we define in this book, notably in Chapters 1 and 2).

4. The project isn't led properly (i.e., there is no trail boss, or the trail boss doesn't fully understand his or her role or can't give the project adequate project management effort).

5. The project is planned properly but then it isn't resourced as was planned (i.e., planned supply and actual supply don't tally).

6. The project is planned such that it has no contingency (i.e., everything has to go *right* on the project for it to be successful).

7. The expectations of project participants aren't managed (i.e., stakeholders are misled as to what they can expect from the project).

8. The project is planned properly but then progress against the plan is not monitored and controlled properly (i.e., we don't follow the plan we laid out).

9. Project reporting is inadequate or nonexistent.

10. When projects get into trouble, people believe the problem can be solved by some simple action (e.g., work harder, extend the deadline, add more resources).

To fix these, all you need to do is go back and ensure that the project managers are carrying out the 10 steps religiously.

External-to-project issues

These are more tricky. These are issues in the wider organization that affect more than one project and need to be fixed by the person who runs the organization.

One of the most common ones here concerns organization-wide supply and demand. Basically, there are not enough people to do everything the organization is trying to do. The result is endless reprioritizing, people moaning about "multiple projects," and fire-fighting.

Another very common one—and I'm sure you don't want to hear this—is about management commitment. Management says one thing but does something different. The case in which management says it is committed to better project management but still imposes impossible missions is still common.

Other issues here involve the management of change. If you are trying to impose more visibility on your projects, then the pain going with this won't be to everyone's liking. You'll get resistance-type issues here.

These are only some of the more common ones. We give some further examples in the case studies in Chapter 16. Whatever they are, they have to be fixed, if your organization is to head toward the heady heights of all-green projects and stay there.

To summarize, it is necessary to do the following:

1. Fix the reds;

2. Clear the blues;

3. Search and destroy oranges;

4. Resolve issues.

The result will be (or should be) a weekly OSR, with an increasing OPI. An example is given in this chapter's User Assistance section, and we will talk more about how to easily generate these weekly OSRs in Chapter 17.

User assistance

Table E (in the color section of this book) gives an example of the output you might get from doing what we have just described.

Notice that the format in Table E is different from those presented in the preceding chapters. This OSR was done using a spreadsheet; in the preceding chapters the OSRs were done with a word processor. There's nothing mysterious about this. OSRs can be as variable as you like—you will see some other variants later in the book—and you should use the tools that work best for you.

To make all the stuff in Chapters 14 and 15 a bit more real, here are a couple of examples.

16 Case Studies

Questions

? Q.1 Your organization is young, growing fast in a high-technology area. An opportunity comes along that could have huge benefits—financially and in terms of growth—for you. The downside is that it will put a huge stress on your finances and your people's ability to cope. You will be so close to the wire, for at least a year, that quite small slip-ups could sink you. What do you do?

(a) Do it anyway—it's what got you where you are.

(b) Pass—it's just too hairy.

(c) Get additional funding to cushion you—giving away equity, if necessary.

(d) Really go for broke. Do this and a few other things besides.

? Q.2 What is the most common reason that project management improvement initiatives fail in organizations?

(a) Lack of management commitment.

(b) Lack of funding.

(c) Reluctance to change on the part of the staff.

(d) Reluctance to invest in project management tools.

? Q.3 If you build a culture of project management in your organization, among its negative effects will be:

(a) The disappearance of "stretch goals"—objectives that really test your people's metal.

(b) Boredom brought on by an almost complete absence of fire-fighting.

(c) Endless time spent creating and updating Gantt charts.

(d) Mind-numbing predictability.

Answers

Q.1
(a) 0 points: This is a book about project management. One of the key things in project management is that the plan should have contingency in it. That's why. (I know there are people out there who'll ignore this one. Fair enough—I've ignored it myself often enough.)
(b) 3 points: It'd probably be better than (a), but it'd be a shame to see the opportunity go. Anyway, what am I worried about? Nobody ever passes on such things.
(c) 5 points: Yep, it's the right answer.
(d) 0 points: Sure, sure. Just keep taking the tablets.

Q.2
(a) 5 points: No question. Management organizes lots of project management training, for example, but continues to hand out impossible missions—or management fails to staff projects adequately.
(b) 4 points: Yes, but generally in the context of (a).
(c) 2 points: It's a problem, but not the biggest one.
(d) 0 points: No way!

Q.3
(a) 0 points: Nope. Objectives can still be set to be challenging.
(b) 0 points: In your dreams! I think you can safely assume there will always be more than enough fire-fighting to go around.
(c) 0 points: Nope. The overhead is nowhere near as high as people like to convince themselves it is. The overhead involved in fire-fighting is always greater—sometimes orders of magnitude greater.
(d) 0 points: That'll be the day!

Scores

11–15 points: Arithmetic not one of your strengths, huh?

1–10 points: Some of these are a matter of style.

0 points: Interesting style!

Introduction

There follow two examples of the application of the ideas we have been talking about.

Case study #1

This first—and very simple—case study is taken from a period in the growth of our own organization. The first OSR gives a picture of the company when we had, for a variety of reasons, drifted a bit from the straight and narrow. This OSR—the result of a hard audit on every project—was taken on November 1 of a particular year and is represented in Table F (in the color section of this book). The OPI is calculated as follows:

- $5 \times$ green $= 5 \times 5 = 25$;
- $3 \times$ orange $= 3 \times 3 = 9$;
- $1 \times$ red $= 1 \times -1 = -1$;
- $8 \times$ blue $= 8 \times 0 = 0$.

The results are thus the following:

- Total score = 33;
- Total projects = 17;
- OPI = 1.9;
- Nine projects at risk. *Note:* We define "projects at risk" to be those projects which are either red (out of control) or blue (have no plan).

In this example, we did things in the following priority order:

- First we fixed the red one—project 9.

- Then we began work on projects 11 and 17 on the basis that neither could wait. The plan for 1998 (project number 17) obviously had an end-of-year deadline, while the investment plan (project number 11) for 1998 was heavily dependent on what investment options we had. Thus it was decided to start these two blues even though we had a red still live.

- When these were sorted out, we moved on the other blues.

Table G (in the color section of this book) depicts the OSR, a little over one month later.

The OPI is calculated as follows:

- $7 \times$ green $= 7 \times 5 = 35$;

- $0 \times$ orange $= 0 \times 3 = 0$;

- $0 \times$ red $= 0 \times -1 = 0$;

- $14 \times$ blue $= 14 \times 0 = 0$.

Therefore, the results are the following:

- Total score = 35;

- Total projects = 21;

- OPI = 1.7;

- Fourteen projects at risk.

The OPI has gone down, and the number of projects at risk has gone up. This is because even though we have removed the red and all of the oranges, a number of new projects came along and had to be added to our list. This very much reflects the real world where new things (projects) are always coming along to take management time and attention. The potential to screw up is essentially greater now.

Table H (in the color section of this book) shows the OSR as it appeared by February 16.

The OPI is calculated as follows:

- $18 \times$ green $= 18 \times 5 = 90$;

- $0 \times$ orange $= 0 \times 3 = 0$;

- $0 \times \text{red} = 0 \times -1 = 0$;

- $6 \times \text{blue} = 6 \times 0 = 0$.

Thus, the results are the following:

- Total score = 90;

- Total projects = 24;

- OPI = 3.8;

- Six projects at risk.

At the risk of boring you, I'll stop at this point. I'm sure you get the idea. Among the OSR's many benefits—I hope you can see—it enables the organization manager to stay focused. We'll talk about this more in Chapter 17. By focusing on—in this case—getting rid of the blues, we ensured that we were always doing the things that most required attention. The next example tries to make this even more apparent.

Case study #2

The case study organization here is a telecommunications company. An initial soft audit was done on 17 projects and yielded the results presented in Table 16.1.

Table 16.1   Case Study #2 OSR

	Initial OSR
Green	3
Orange	5
Blue	1
Red	8
OPI	1.3
At risk	9

While this picture presented by Table 16.1 is not very good, the reality is generally worse. In a soft audit, greens may not always be on target—project managers can delude themselves into thinking they are, but a hard audit often proves otherwise. Equally, and for the same reason, oranges often turn out to be reds.

Two months later, another hard audit shows a considerable improvement (Table 16.2). Table 16.2 shows a dramatic increase in the number of greens and a reduction in the number of reds. Also, no project is without a plan now.

Table 16.2   Improved OSR, Case Study #2

	Initial OSR	After 2 months
Green	3	9
Orange	5	5
Blue	1	0
Red	8	3
OPI	1.3	3.4
At risk	9	3

In making this transition, the following were the issues that emerged and would have to be solved for the organization to go forward and improve its project management still further. In no particular order, they were the following:

1. Project managers not taking ownership of projects: People having the title but no clear idea of what that implied for them.

2. Some projects having no project managers.

3. Inadequate resourcing: Supply not equal to demand on some projects.

4. Some projects with no plans.

5. Some projects with plans that contained no contingency.

6. No project tracking: Very few project plans tracked against and updated with any kind of regularity.

7. No or ineffective status reporting: At best status reports were of the "day-at-the-beach" variety.

How to run your organization effectively and still find time for the things that matter.

17 The Lazy Manager's Weekly Routine

Questions

? Q.1 Your natural management style is one of micromanagement, where you want to know the detail on everything. You have a superstar manager reporting to you. By this I mean he or she is totally reliable—just give him or her the job and you can consider it done. What management style should you use in these circumstances?

(a) Your natural one. A leopard can't change its spots.

(b) As in (a) but do so with the intention of learning how he or she does it, so you can see if you can pass that learning onto others.

(c) Leave him or her to it.

(d) Go with micromanagement—just to be sure.

? Q.2 Your natural management style is to let somebody get on with the job. Your favorite saying is "What's the point in having a dog and barking yourself?" (In these politically correct times, you don't actually say this around the office!) You hire a new manager to work for you. At the interview, you ask this manager straight out if he or she is the kind of person who, when you give him or her a job to do, you can consider it done. Without hesitation, he or she answers "yes." What management style is right here?

(a) Micromanagement—you've never worked with this person before.

(b) Your natural style—it's the perfect match.

(c) Something part-way between (a) and (b).

(d) Micromanagement to begin with and then back off when you see he or she is doing okay.

? Q.3   You have somebody working for you who has ended up in a job that he or she is really not capable of doing. You have a lot of personal loyalty to him or her, and the organization could "carry" this person without too much financial or other disruption. The person would lose a lot of face if you were to remove him or her. What do you do?

(a) Move this person to a job he or she can do.

(b) Just leave things as they are. If it ain't broke, don't fix it.

(c) Try and get the person to see the situation for himself or herself and have *him or her* offer to make the move to another job.

(d) It's an HR problem. Give it to the folks in HR.

Answers

Q.1
(a) 0 points: Well, you'd better—because if you don't change your spots, your manager will change his or her job!
(b) 0 points: First, he or she won't see it like that. Second, if you've got that kind of time on your hands, I'm sure there's something more useful you could be doing with yourself.
(c) 5 points: Yep.
(d) 0 points: If you go with the micromanagement, your manager will go. Think about it.

Q.2
(a) 0 points: Don't think so. If this manager's as reliable as claimed, this isn't going to be a happy start to your working relationship.

(b) 0 points: To paraphrase an old saying, "There are lies, damned lies, and what people tell you at interviews." Supposing the superstar turns out to be a duffer?

(c) 5 points: "Okay, so what do I do, Mister Smartypants?" I hear you say, in exasperation. Well, this, actually: Without being too intrusive, see how he or she is doing. If he or she has a deadline for a particular job, check some while in advance that it is where you would expect it to be. If it is not, you can move closer to the micromanagement. If it is, you can slide back to your natural style.

(d) 0 points: This answer is a bit similar to answer (c), except it has the downside of answer (a). I think (c) is better.

Q.3

(a) 5 points: Only answer, in my view.

(b) 0 points: Don't think so. Taking the long view, nobody will thank you for it, not the person, not that person's colleagues and peers, not your management. Being nice doesn't always lead to nice results.

(c) 5 points: Always worth a try. If it works it's a happy outcome for everybody.

(d) 0 points: No, it's not. It's your problem. This is why they pay you your salary.

Scores

11–15 points: Nice sensitivity to and adjustment of style to suit the circumstances.

5–10 points: Okay, I agree it's not 100% black and white.

Less than 5: In other words, zero: It's not this fuzzy.

Introduction

In my previous book [1], I introduced the concept of the "lazy project manager." This was the idea that you could do the least amount of work possible and still have a successful outcome to your project. It was the idea of knowing—and being confident—that you had done enough project management work on your project. We called it the "lazy project manager," but *lazy* was used in a highly complimentary, rather than a derogatory, sense.

(I think the use of the word *lazy* like this has certainly thrown some people. I had one person phone me up saying they really liked my idea of the "dumb project manager"!)

The previous book described daily and weekly routines that the project manager could follow. The purpose of these was to try to make the behavior change required by structured project management easy to implement. The payback for those who applied these routines was that they found themselves making much more effective and efficient use of their time—of their days and weeks.

This chapter tries to do something similar for the organization manager—abbreviated here to simply "the manager."

The basic concept is that the manager uses his or her OSR as instrumentation to "drive" the organization. The OSR can be described as follows:

- It is updated, based on what is happening in the "world" (i.e., in the organization).

- It points you back into the world to where attention is required.

The weekly routine runs from Monday to Friday, assuming that all projects submit their status reports by close of business the previous Friday. The weekly routine works in an endless "update OSR—go do it" loop as described in the following section.

The weekly routine

Here's how you might organize your week.

Monday

Come in. Get those little morning rituals out of the way—the first cup (or mug, or flagon, or IV drip) of coffee, the 10-mile run, that sort of thing.

Update OSR

To update the OSR, do the following.

1. Now open your OSR.

2. Update it on the basis of any status reports that have come in.

3. If there is no status report, consider it orange.

4. Issue this as your status report for the week just finished. OSRs are intended to be largely self-evident. You may, however, want to attach an explanatory commentary to particular parts of it. (Remember not to overwrite OSR values but instead to keep them from week to week. This is knowledge management in action. See Table E for an illustration of what I mean.)

5. Now begin your new week's work as described in the following subsection.

Go do it

Generate your to-do list. Do this in the following manner:

- Identify actions required to fix any reds (rescues followed by scoping and planning);

- Identify actions required to fix any blues (scoping and planning);

- Identify actions required to fix any oranges (hard audits);

- Identify any projects about which you are jumpy, launching hard audits and then fixing the resulting issues.

Subsequently, do items on the to-do list in the priority described above. Note that some items on the to-do list may be very quick—hold a meeting, send an e-mail, and so forth. Others may turn out to be little (or even large) projects in their own right. For the latter, treat it exactly as a project (i.e., generate the list of jobs and start working the list as described in Part One). When you have progressed each of the items as much as you can that day, you're done for the day. Then, you can turn the page of your diary (I mean this quite literally) and start doing tomorrow's work (i.e., doing the progressing that you would have done tomorrow). In our trail boss analogy, this is the equivalent to riding on ahead of the herd looking for trouble.

Update OSR

As items complete, feed results back into OSR.

Tuesday–Friday

These are almost identical to Mondays apart from the issuing of the status report. Just continue to work your to-do list and update your OSR (i.e., continue the "update OSR—go do it" cycle).

If you've stayed with it this far, here are all the things you have to do to make your organization run as a project-based organization.

18 Program for a Project-Based Organization

Questions

Q.1 You've just joined a new organization. After a few weeks observing, you decide that significant parts of its senior management are dysfunctional, incompetent, and really not up to what is being asked of them. What do you do?

(a) Wade in with the ax.

(b) Try to understand the problems and launch a program of staff and team development.

(c) Begin micromanaging and mentoring the wayward ones.

(d) It's an HR problem—give it to them, and if they won't take it, quit.

Q.2 Of the following list, which is the one that your people most want of you, the one that will gain their respect and cause them to follow you through the fires of hell and back?

(a) Telling them what's going on—where the organization is going and their part in it.

(b) Top-of-the-range salaries and other benefits.

(c) A good working environment and fancy tools.

(d) That you seem to have all the answers about where the organization is heading.

? Q.3 Of the following list, which is the one that your customers most want of you?

(a) Low prices.

(b) A cool Web site.

(c) That, good or bad, they know how they stand.

(d) That you deliver on your commitments.

Answers

Q.1
(a) 3 points: You're in a bad situation, and none of these answers is particularly right or wrong. This one? I've done it; it's no fun; and you'd better make sure that, at the very least, your solution doesn't make things worse. If it does, you may as well go yourself.

(b) 3 points: Three points for this because you're taking the view that whatever's broken can be fixed. Maybe you're right. Sure, I can imagine you went home one night and said to your significant other "pack of bloody incompetents," but maybe you'll find out that with a bit of help, they're not.

(c) 3 points: Might work. The danger, of course, is that it starts to soak up so much of your time that you start to flounder. Then you're all doomed.

(d) 0 points: Zero points if you said it's an HR problem. It's not. Quit? Zero points for that too because I'd like to think you're made of sterner stuff.

Q.2
(a) 5 points: And the nice thing is it's free! All it takes is some of your time. Obviously, there may be some things you can't say, so we're not saying to tell them 100%—but we could all tell our troops a lot more, and it wouldn't hurt a bit.

(b) 0 points: They won't object, but that's not the top one.

(c) 0 points: They won't object, but that's not the top one either.

(d) 0 points: Naw! That wouldn't impress me—would it you?

Q.3

(a) 0 points: They won't object, but that's not the answer.

(b) 0 points: Now, you knew that wasn't right.

(c) 4 points: Yes.

(d) 5 points: But clearly, they'd rather this!

Scores

12–13 points: Nice. You've got a very clear view of the world. (Unless, that is, you think you scored 14 or 15!)

5–11 points: Sure, this is a good score.

Less than 5: Well, maybe you got the first one or the last one right.

Introduction

If you want to become a "project-based organization" or "a project management-based culture," there are seven things you have to do. The next section says what they are. The section after that gives a little plan for implementing them.

The seven things

The seven things are the following:

1. Find an approach.

2. Train practitioners in the approach.

3. Find some tools that support the approach.

4. Build a database of previous projects with which the tools interact.

5. Enforce the approach.

6. Write standard operating procedures for project managers.

7. Educate the rest of the organization.

These steps are described in the following subsections.

Find an approach

There are many out there. All the big consultancy firms and many smaller ones have their own—watch out for words like *methodology*. Your key issues here should be the following:

1. Is there a clear correlation between use of the approach (methodology) and successful projects?

2. Where does the approach lie on a scale of, at one end, common sense, and at the other, rocket science? The closer it is to rocket science, the more circumspect I'd be. From the point of view of this book, we gave you the approach in Chapter 1.

Train practitioners

Once you've chosen the methodology, you need to train the project managers in its use. Any training needs to be more about behavior change and less about Gantt charts and PERT charts. The training also needs to be able to deal with three of the fundamental problems in project management:

1. How can I predict the future (also known as project planning)?

2. How can I make that prediction come true (project execution)?

3. Can I know if I've been given an impossible mission and, if so, what should I do in those circumstances? (This one is where the behavior change is most vital.)

Part One describes some of the things practitioners have to be able to do.

Find some tools

In general, the simpler the tool the better. If you can get away with pen and paper, why use a computer? If a spreadsheet will do the business, what's the point in grappling with a project management tool? On the other hand, for many projects, project management tools deal accurately with large volumes of project data that would be impossible to process any other way. This book has given you some simple tools.

Build a database of previous projects with which the tools interact

No two projects are the same—but neither is every project completely different from every other project. Yet many people behave as though their project were completely different from every other project that has ever been done in that organization or in that area of technology.

Given that project management *is* about predicting the future, failing to learn from the past is one of the surest ways to get it wrong again in the future. On the other hand, storing templates, estimates, and other project performance information from previous projects ensures that we can draw on this knowledge when we come to plan and execute our next project. These days it's become fashionable all over again—it's called "knowledge management." Yep, we talked about it in Chapter 9.

Enforce the approach

Just because you gave people a training course doesn't mean that everything will suddenly be transformed. Call it "reinforcement," "support," "monitoring," or some other politically correct term if you wish, but you need to ensure that the new ways of doing things become embedded in the organization. Most of Part Two is about giving you the techniques to carry out enforcement.

Standard operating procedures

One of the best ways of embedding the new ethos is to give the project managers a "bible," a set of procedures or manual, describing "how project management is done around here." I'd like to think that this book could be used as the basis for some of these so that you wouldn't be starting from a blank sheet of paper.

Educate the rest

Use education—as opposed to training. By this I mean spreading the word throughout the organization, to management, to the troops, so that everybody knows the nature of the culture change that's taking place.

Apart from buying more copies of the book—and feel free to do so!—the best way of educating the rest is to have them see and experience the results of "doing it right."

Little implementation plan

Figure 18.1 depicts an implementation plan.

Figure 18.1
Implementation plan.

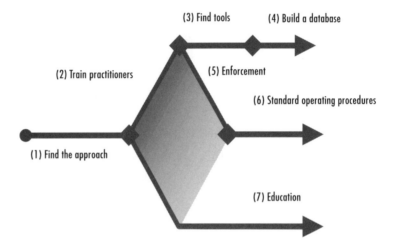

Notes on the implementation plan:

1. Nothing can start until you've done this.

2. Yeah, let's start seeing some results right away. The lengths of the bars are not to scale, so that this can be done relatively quickly. Implied is the fact that new practitioners also get trained.

3. If you wanted to, you could begin this earlier—as soon as (1) ends. To keep the diagram simple, I've assumed you find a tool set and start to use these. Presumably, in reality, you'll always be searching for the better mousetrap.

4. This depends on at least one project ending. After that it is a continuous process.

5. Enforcement has to begin as soon as training ends and must continue, in some shape or form, as long as the organization continues.

6. In theory, this can be started as soon as training ends and updated after that. In reality, you're probably better off waiting until the tools and the database are in place. I've shown it as an ongoing activity because while the writing of them isn't, keeping them current is.

7. Can start as soon as the approach is chosen—and you can never do enough of it.

PART THREE
Treating Your Organization as a Project

In Part Three, the book shows how, by treating your whole organization as a project, you can derive maximum benefit from the ideas and techniques described thus far. Chapter 19 is about building the plan in these circumstances, and Chapter 20 is about executing the plan.

It may seem complicated, but it's not. In this chapter we show how it is possible to build a plan for your entire organization using the techniques we have learned already.

19 Building the Plan

Questions

Q.1 You've just joined a new organization. It is ISO 9000 certified, so lots of procedures are documented. PC-based project management tools are in widespread use. Projects are the way everything is done, and people are committed to this notion. Everyone feels that the organization's project management "could be improved a bit," so you decide to buy in some training. Your direct reports assure you that, if you come up with the training money, that should tie all of the different project management elements—procedures, tools, processes, people—in place. What do you do?

(a) Tell them their analysis is wrong and that, in your experience, training has never had this kind of effect in any organization.

(b) It makes sense—go ahead with off-the-shelf training.

(c) It makes sense—go ahead with the training but have it tailored to your organization.

(d) It makes sense—go ahead with the training, but find the best that money can buy and then have it tailored to your organization.

Q.2 What are the benefits of treating your organization as a project?

(a) Solves resource conflicts upfront rather than when they happen.

(b) Enables you to understand where your management team needs strengthening.

(c) Ensures that your business strategy and operational programs complement one another.

(d) Provides you a highly sensitive early warning system.

? Q.3 What are the disadvantages of treating your organization as a project?

(a) It'll take too much time and effort.

(b) It'll make things too predictable and remove all the "fire" from the organization.

(c) The trouble with planning is that you never know when you've done enough or when to stop. We'll have that problem here.

(d) We'll be swamped with detail.

Answers

Q.1
(a) 5 points: Not in my experience, either.
(b) 0 points: You weren't paying attention when you read Chapter 18.
(c) 0 points: It's better, but it still won't have the effect they're promising.
(d) 0 points: Nor will this.

Q.2
(a) 5 points: Yep.
(b) 5 points: Yep.
(c) 5 points: Yep.
(d) 5 points: Yep.

Q.3
(a) 0 points: We'll try to show you that it won't.
(b) 0 points: You're kidding, right? I'd give you –5 if I could.
(c) 0 points: Don't think so. I think we'll be able to show that it will be fairly self-evident when to stop.
(d) 0 points: Again, we'll stop at the right place, and whatever detail there is will be carefully structured, so that you can see both the forest and the trees.

Scores

10 or more points: Okay, you seem pretty open to what we're going to do.

1–9 points: Read on.

0 points: Maybe you should have bought a different book.

Introduction

In her book *The Seven Deadly Sins of Business* [10], Eileen Shapiro lists as one the "sins of strategy," organizations that make the mistake of creating a vision but not giving any clear direction as to how that vision is to be achieved. The result is that the organization often develops in ways that the strategists hadn't intended. By treating your organization as a project and planning it as we have previously described, you avoid that situation.

There is a concept I've sometimes seen referred to as "breakthrough thinking." Like many of these things, it's probably just a new-fangled name for an old-fashioned idea. The idea is that to build your strategic plan, you first imagine where you want to be. Imagine yourself standing there. Next imagine that you can look back toward where you actually are. Now ask yourself the question "How did I get to be here?" This will enable you to build both your vision and your plan. This is essentially what we're going to do here.

In this chapter, we apply scoping and planning, as described in Chapter 2, to our organization. We describe the application of each of the planning steps in turn. Each of the steps is illustrated in this chapter's User Assistance section. We conclude the chapter with a brief discussion on how much effort is likely to go into an exercise like this.

Step 1: Visualize the goal

One of the problems with the way many organizational plans are built at the moment is that each department or section builds its own piece of the plan, its budget, and so on. Then all the individual plans are sucked into a big machine, some great wheels turn, all sorts of compromises get made, and conflicts get resolved (yeah, sure they do!). Ultimately, the final plan rolls out the other side.

How to Run Successful High-Tech Project-Based Organizations

A different way to approach it is to first of all identify what you are trying to achieve. What do you want life to be like when the project ends? This has always been our key goal-setting question. To answer it for your organization, do the following:

1. Set the point you are trying to plan to as an artificial "end" of the project. For example, if you are trying to do the calendar 1999 plan, then the "end" of the project is December 31, 1999 (or earlier if, like in many parts of Europe, things pretty much close down from about mid-December onward).

2. Now ask yourself all the Chapter 2 questions, based around this date as the end of the project. This will enable you to build your goal, or your vision of what you want your organization to be like on that chosen day. This chapter's User Assistance section shows an example. You can improve on your basic vision—if you want to think of it like that—by taking a second pass at it as follows.

3. Suppose your planning horizon were for a year—let's say you were doing the calendar 1999 plan, and you had planned up to December 31, 1999. A good thing to do would be to come back to your work a few days later, when it had all had a chance to settle and go through the process again. This time, though, pick December 31, 2000, as your horizon and pretend that you stand at December 31, 1999, with all of your 1999 objectives achieved.

4. Now imagine what you would want your December 31, 2000, vision to look like, using again the Chapter 2 questions. What this will almost invariably throw up for you is things that you need to start *now* in order for them to become a reality in 2000.

5. Obviously you can repeat this process more times, if you think that makes sense. Personally, I couldn't see you getting much value out of more than three.

Now you could argue that the straightforward three- and five-year strategic plan would have the same effect as what we just described. I would argue that it wouldn't. With the traditional strategic plans, you are much more likely to get the discontinuity that Shapiro talked about in her book.

In addition, a concept that I have come across recently and that I really like is the idea of "Web time" and, in particular, a "Web year." The idea is that everything changes so quickly on the Web that the effect is almost as though what used to take a year now seems to happen in about three months. You've guessed it. A "Web year" is considered to be three months. Thus, four Web years fit into a conventional calendar year. The reason I mention this is because, in my view, three- and five-year plans in this day and age are comparable to trying to predict 12–20 years ahead. Forget it, I'd say. Year and two-year horizons should be more than enough for most situations. Three is pushing it, I would say.

There is a thing we should mention here called "scenario analysis." It's quite possible that events could actually unfold in one of a number of different ways ("scenarios"). Having built one plan, it's then a pretty straightforward job to use that plan to build plans (models) of the other possible scenarios. (Note that this is essentially the "flavors" of the plan idea that we saw in Chapter 1.) The act of building each plan should enable you to identify "early warning signs" for that particular scenario. Then, if you pick up the signs that a particular scenario is starting to unfold, you can switch to that version of the plan.

Given that some people rarely produce *one* plan, it's probably pushing it to ask them to produce a few. However, if you have built one plan, then it will certainly serve as a benchmark to determine how closely unfolding events are following the plan, or how far they are from it. If you find that you are in a significantly different scenario from that which you had originally envisaged, you can still use the plan at that stage to generate a new scenario.

Step 2: List of jobs

Each of the elements in the goal statement will only happen if a set of jobs are put in place to make it happen. Thus the elements in the goal statement are the springboard for building the list of jobs. In addition, there are some "don't forget" types of things that occur in many organizations—for example, an administration function —and these also require jobs to make them happen.

Having listed the jobs, we then have to identify any dependencies between jobs and estimate the effort involved in the jobs. It's enough to do these estimates of effort in units like person-months. I certainly wouldn't go to any smaller units at this top-level stage. As always, estimates are arrived at by trying to either arrive at some detail or by using assumptions or both. An example of a set of jobs and associated efforts is given in the User Assistance section. (The total effort identified is 468 person-months.)

Step 3: One leader

Here you are concerned with three issues:

- That each individual piece has a trail boss;

- That the project as a whole has a trail boss;

- That you calculate the project management effort required for the project as a whole and for each of the pieces.

To take the top question first, what you actually want to do here is establish an organization structure that will help you manage the pieces. In choosing a structure, your concern will not be about whether the structure should be flat or hierarchical or matrix or anything else. Your guiding principle will be that each piece has somebody to trail-boss it. The following steps will help you establish an organization structure:

1. An easy way to achieve this is to group the sets of jobs into logical pieces. (You'll find that lots of them are already in logical groupings or fit naturally together anyway.) Subsequently, ensure that each of the groupings has a trail boss.

2. Make all these trail bosses report to one overall trail boss.

3. Now calculate the effort required by each of the trail bosses, using the 10% rule of thumb. This will tell you whether everyone is the following:

- Just right;

- Overloaded—then part of what they're trail-bossing needs to be moved to somebody else;

- Underutilized—then they are a contender to take somebody's overload. Alternatively, they are free to do jobs on some part of some project as well as being a trail boss.

Step 4: Assign people to jobs

Now that we have the demand—468 person-months, as identified in step 2—we need to match supply to it. The easiest way to do this is use a spreadsheet and enter onto it the people who will carry out the various jobs from step 2. The User Assistance section continues our example in Table 19.1.

Having gotten to this point, we now have our basic supply-demand model. For an organization, even more so than a project, the next key question to be asked is what it all is going to cost.

Almost always in projects, we represent the plan/supply-demand model as a Gantt chart. This is a "who does what when" representation of the plan. We can also, however, represent the plan in a "who spends/earns what when" form (i.e., in a spreadsheet). This is therefore what we do next. The example continues in the User Assistance section in Table 19.2.

Step 5(a): Contingency

The plan must have contingency. It does. Apart from that already mentioned regarding the overall trail boss having half her time free as contingency, there is also a line item in the spreadsheet labeled "Contingency."

Clearly there are other contingencies too. This organization is indeed beginning an expansion, fueled by its cash flow. Should it turn out that the cash flow is not happening as per the plan, then obviously hiring plans will be slowed, as will the office move that was talked about. We should also do a risk analysis, and we show one for our example in the User Assistance section.

Step 5(b): Manage expectations

We have now made one complete pass through Steps 1–5(a), the project scoping and planning steps. We may be completely happy with what we have achieved. On the other hand, we might feel that there is room for fine-tuning, or we may want to ask "what if" types of questions.

Our model—in this case, represented in spreadsheet form—enables us to do exactly that. If you remember, in the example in the User Assistance section at the end of this chapter, the profit target had fallen significantly short of what we had originally hoped for in our goal setting. We can now use the model to see if that shortfall can be improved upon—or maybe we're happy with the profit margin in the model, given all the expansion we are doing. Whatever our situation, we have options about which version of the plan we eventually go forward with. Note that any options generated will result in a reiteration of steps 1–5.

Finally, we do the following:

- Document the plan;

- Present the plan to the organization—both delivering some form of presentation and giving them a copy of the document to take away and consider.

Clearly, this is the top-level organizational plan. We will now expect the individual trail bosses to go away and produce plans for their own pieces, exactly as we have described here. How many levels there are and how many plans will depend on whether we are General Electric or a "mom and pop" company.

So how much work is involved in producing one of these plans?

I guess the first (pretty subjective) answer to this question is to look in the User Assistance section. I hope when you do, you'll see that all of this could be done relatively quickly and without any great difficulty. The key, as always, is to involve the people who will do the work.

A second, more quantitative answer, is to take a rule of thumb I've tended to use for a long time, which is that building such a plan will take about one-quarter of one percent of the total effort in the plan. Thus, the plan in the User Assistance example contains 39 person-years worth of effort. This is 468 person-months. One percent of that is 4.6 person-months. A quarter of that is 1.15 person-months, which is about 23 person-days. This might be broken down as follows:

- Initial brainstorming on steps 1, 2, 3 (5–7 people for a day): 5–7 person-days (PD);

- Document results (one person for two days): 2 PD;

- Second brainstorming to review and finalize plan (5–7 people for a day): 5–7 PD;

- Final document (one person for two days): 2 PD;

- Present to rest of organization (40 people for two hours): 5 PD;

- Total: 24–28 PD.

I've used this rule of thumb for a long time now, and it seems to be pretty valid, independent of the size of the organization or project. The key, of course, is to go to an appropriate level of detail and not to get bogged down by going too low. The example that follows tries to show you a level of detail that's about right. In addition, if you find yourself getting snarled up in things and suddenly thinking that instead of your one-day off-site brainstorming, you're now going to need at least a week, then you've probably gone too low. I'm fully convinced that no matter what the size or complexity of your organization, the following statement is true. If you can't put some high-level shape on your organization in a day—by which I mean a vision and a first-cut supply-demand plan, no matter how rough—then you probably have some fundamental problems that you're going to need more than a book on project management to sort out!

User assistance

This section contains a complete example of the things we have been talking about.

Step 1: Visualize the goal

Here, first of all, is the kind of material that might come straight off the flip chart at your scoping session. The material is for an imaginary organization—in this case, a small company.

Goals

- Profitable—quantify exactly;

- Product mix of 30% As and 70% Bs;

- Financially secure (i.e., cash in the bank and with options);

- Dividend(?);

- Market-driven (market-driven implies technological innovation);

- Consolidate (i.e., get what we're doing right before we move on);

- Fun;

- Clear structure and reporting lines and communications;

- Facilities improved;

- Adequate time allotted to project management;

- Strengthen management as individuals and as a team;

- Proper financial system (including Europe);

- Core values formalized and company runs accordingly;

- Longer strategy in place as regards realizing shareholder value (get stock valued?);

- Move from people-centered to process-centered—in terms of delivery (packaging, people);

- Brand management;

- Coherent IS strategy/delivery in place and being implemented and supporting cohesion;

- Admin.—growth with company/measure/improvement;

- Employee handbook;

- Pension scheme;

- Clarity in remuneration;

- Cohesion of "team";

- Worthy causes;

- Ensure company is of benefit to the community;

- Product development;

- Maintain growth (QUANTIFY);

- Meet sales targets;

- Standardize delivery;

- Hold all people;

- Maintain ISO accreditation;

- Company number one in our market sector.

Now, here is how such material might get processed into a goal visualization.

On Friday, December 17, 1999, our company will look like this (in no particular order):

- Revenues of $2.75M and profits of $0.5 M. (There is more detail in the financial forecasts of this plan.) There will be money in the bank at least equal to the accounts receivable amount.

- Everyone will agree that we've had a real blast of a year. Staff turnover will be no more than 10%.

- We will have moved to more spacious and better equipped offices.

- We will have given away 50 days of effort to good causes.

- There will be a clear path to the realization of shareholder value in 2000.

- The IS facilities, infrastructure, and added value will have taken a quantum leap.

- The pension scheme and employee handbook will be in place.

- A marketing information system will be driving everything. In particular, recognition of our brand will have increased significantly over the year, and we will be company number one in our sector.

- Our team will be much more cohesive as a unit.

- We will continue to be ISO 9000 compliant.

- Everyone in the company will have had at least five days formal training.

Step 2: List of jobs

The following checklist provides an example of a list of jobs derived from the goal visualization work done in step 1. Apart from the goal statement elements, which generate sets of jobs, there are also jobs like "admin." or "financial" that are likely to be part of many organizations. In the list, "PM" indicates person-month.

1 Complete plan and sign off (2 PM);

❑ Complete planning session;
❑ Write up;
❑ Review plan ourselves;
❑ November 2 presentation to all staff;
❑ Update;
❑ Review;
❑ Sign off.

2 Profitable (101 PM)

2.1 Marketing information system (including brand management) (18 PM)
❑ Market research (172 PD + 10% = 10 PM);

❏ Marketing information system (4 PM; ¼ of somebody's time);
❏ Sales and promotions (4 PM).

2.2 Do the sales targets (1 PM)
2.3 Projections and cash flow (10 PM)
2.4 Meet sales targets (6 people 12 PM = 72 PM)

3 Fun (4 PM)

3.1 Christmas party (1 PM)
3.2 BBQ II (1 PM)
3.3 T-shirt competition II (0 PM)
3.4 Core values (1 PM)

4 Structure/reporting lines/communication (10 PM)

❏ Determine, publish, and keep updated the organization structure (1 PM);
❏ Complete and distribute the 1999 plan (3 PM);
❏ Ensure company-wide status reports issued weekly (2 PM);
❏ Hold staff meetings (1 PM);
❏ Identify and carry out other ways of improving communications company-wide (3 PM).

5 Facilities (9 PM)

5.1 Short-term solution (25 PD)
5.2 Long-term solution (155 PD)—our effort in planning and making the move

6 Financial (12 PM)

Proper system for:
❏ Budgeting (6 PM);
❏ Control (3 PM);
❏ Reporting (3 PM):
  • Departmental;
  • Project.

7 Core values/benefits to the community (5 PM)

❑ Finalize core values/distribute/keep updated (1 PM);
❑ Make them part of the appraisal process (1 PM);
❑ Identify and implement worthy causes (3 PM)—block of days available to worthy causes.

8 Product delivery (165 PM)

❑ Validate documented process (2 PM);
❑ How we deliver programs (6 PM);
❑ QA (9 PM);
❑ Delivery (124 PM);
❑ Consultant administration (4 PM);
❑ Internal project delivery and account management and sales support (20 PM).

9 IS strategy (40 PM)

❑ Agree on it;
❑ Complete plan;
❑ Review;
❑ Update;
❑ Sign off;
❑ Review results.

10 admin. (67 PM)

❑ Lisa, Maggie (24 PM);
❑ Viki (12 PM);
❑ Requirements are:

  • One extra person immediately (12 PM);

  • One extra person in Q2 (9 PM);

  • One extra person in Q2 (9 PM).

❑ Hire and train them (1 PM).

11 Product development (24 PM)

❑ Will feed into branding (24 PM) assuming
two people @ 12 PM.

12 Human resources (19 PM)

❑ Recruitment (12 extra people @ 5 PD per person =
3 PM);
❑ Develop employee handbook (3 PM);
❑ Training plans/programs (50 × 1 PD; say, 3 PM);
❑ Pension scheme (install and run) (1 PM);
❑ Stock option scheme (1 PM);
❑ Remuneration sorted (2 PM);
❑ Appraisals (50 × 2 × 1 PD = 5 PM);
❑ Health and safety (1 PM).

13 Legal (1 PM)

❑ Ensure all requirements satisfied (1 PM).

14 QA (includes ISO 9002) (9 PM)

14.1 ISO 9002 (Retain/maintain/develop) (2 PM)
14.2 Identify what they are (1 PM)
14.3 Do it (6 PM)

The checklist total is 468 PM.

Step 3: One leader

The jobs in the previous section could be grouped into five
categories:

- Sales and marketing (jobs 2);

- Human resources, legal, admin., finance, and facilities (jobs
  3, 5, 6, 10, 12, 13);

- Product development and delivery (jobs 8, 11, 14);

- IS (jobs 9);

- Overall management (jobs 1, 4, 7).

Thus:

- Sales and marketing (101 PM);

- Human resources, legal, admin., finance, and facilities (112 PM);

- Product development and delivery (198 PM);

- IS (40 PM);

- Overall management (17 PM).

So, taking 10% of each of these:

- Sales and marketing (10 PM)—almost a full-time job.

- HR, legal, admin., finance, and facilities (11.2 PM) —definitely a full-time job.

- Product development and delivery (19.8 PM)—work enough for nearly two people. This implies that we will have to build a structure inside or outside product development and delivery to spread the management load. Let's say we decide to split product delivery from product development and QA.

- IS (4 PM)—one person a third of the time (i.e., about 1½–2 days per week.

- Overall management (1.7 PM)—but let's come back to this in a moment.

Therefore, here is a structure that might suggest itself for the overall trail boss:

- Sales and marketing trail boss—full-time;

- HR, legal, admin., finance, facilities trail boss—full-time;

- Product delivery (at 16.5 PM there is still more load spreading to be done here)—full-time;

- Product development and QA (3.3—maybe this person can take another piece of product delivery and even the load more). Let's assume that he or she can take the 4.5 PM surplus, thus reducing the other person to 12 PM (i.e., one person full-time for the year) and raising them to 7.8 PM (i.e., two-thirds of the time or 3–4 days per week) —two-thirds of the time;

- IS—one-third of the time.

The overall trail boss must run a group consisting of four equivalent people—the three full-timers, the two-thirds person, and the one-third person. This is the equivalent of having a 4 person-person-year = 48 PM project to run. Adding in the 17 PM gets you to 65 PM. Taking 10% of this gives 6.5 PM, which means that—on paper, at least—running this organization is roughly a half-time job.

So what does our hero do the rest of the time? Well, I guess these calculations assume a perfect world where everybody is doing their jobs properly. In reality, the rest of the time is contingency for the following:

- Fire-fighting, when subordinates screw up or for other reasons.

- New things that invariably will come along. (Without contingency, we'd be assuming that nothing unexpected is going to happen to this organization over the next year. That's a really smart assumption, I think you'll agree!)

- Gazing out the window and trying to see the future—and if you got to spend nearly half your year doing exactly that, I'd be prepared to bet that your organization would benefit mightily from such activity.

Clearly, lots of other organization structures are possible in this example. The important things we have achieved here are these:

- All pieces have somebody responsible for them.

- Everybody has been allowed adequate time to do their management tasks.

These accomplishments are exactly what Chapter 2 required us to do.

Step 4: Assign people to jobs

A spreadsheet representation of the people assignments is shown in Table 19.1. Please note the following about Table 19.1.

1. The numbers under sales and marketing are read from job 2 (entitled "profitable") in the list of jobs. One and a half marketing people are required, six sales people, and a trail boss. Looking at the 11 PM for "sales targets, projections, and cash flow," we discover that this is a duplication of "6 financial,"

Table 19.1   People Assignments

Group/project	Staff Allocations — 1999												Who
	Jan	Feb	Mar	Apr	May	Jun	Jul	Aug	Sep	Oct	Nov	Dec	
The ACME Company													
Overall trail boss	1	1	1	1	1	1	1	1	1	1	1	1	
Sales and Marketing													
Trail boss	1	1	1	1	1	1	1	1	1	1	1	1	
Sales	6	6	6	6	6	6	6	6	6	6	6	6	
Marketing	1.5	1.5	1.5	1.5	1.5	1.5	1.5	1.5	1.5	1.5	1.5	1.5	
HR/Admin./Legal/Facilities/Finance													
Trail boss & 1 legal	1	1	1	1	1	1	1	1	1	1	1	1	
3 Fun/5 facilities	1	1	1	1	1	1	1	1	1	1	1	1	
6 Finance	1	1	1	1	1	1	1	1	1	1	1	1	
10 Admin													
	2	2	2	2	2	2	2	2	2	2	2	2	Lisa, Maggie
	1	1	1	1	1	1	1	1	1	1	1	1	Viki
	1	1	1	1	1	1	1	1	1	1	1	1	New hire
				2	2	2	2	2	2	2	2	2	New hire
11 HR	1.5	1.5	1.5	1.5	1.5	1.5	1.5	1.5	1.5	1.5	1.5	1.5	
8 Product Delivery													
Trail boss	1	1	1	1	1	1	1	1	1	1	1	1	
Staff	9	9	9	9	11	11	11	16	16	16	18	18	
Contractors	1	1	1	1	1	1	1	1	1	1	1	1	
Trail boss	1	1	1	1	1	1	1	1	1	1	1	1	
11 Product development	2	2	2	2	2	2	2	2	2	2	2	2	
14 QA				1	1	1	1	1	1	1	1	1	
9 IS	3	3	3	3	3	3	3	3	3	3	3	3	
	35	35	35	38	40	40	40	45	45	45	47	47	

and so we make a decision to eliminate the former on the basis that this more sensibly belongs elsewhere.

2. Again, for HR/admin./legal/facilities/finance, the numbers of person-months in the job list are converted into people in the spreadsheet. (I know the number of support people probably looks out of whack here—but it's intended just to illustrate the technique. Or—if you won't buy that—let's assume that this organization is about to embark on a major expansion and is putting all of these people in place to provide a solid base for the expansion.) The 1 PM for "hire and train them" is probably already covered in "12 human resources" in the job list.

3. For "8 product delivery" we can read the numbers from the list of jobs and consider how quickly we might feasibly ramp up this department.

4. This happens again for "11 product development," "14 QA," and "9 IS"; and these are grouped under a trail boss, as we had proposed earlier.

The spreadsheet in Table 19.1 now represents the first cut of our supply part of the organizational supply-demand equation.

A spreadsheet representation of the plan is shown in Table 19.2.

The cash flow in Table 19.2 shows a revenue of $2.45M and a profit of $318K. Note that these are slightly lower—in the case of the revenue—and much lower—in the case of the profit—than the targets we set ourselves in the original goal/vision statement. We deal with this issue in step 5(b) (see above).

Step 5(a): Contingency

Table 19.3 presents a risk analysis for our example.

Table 19.2   Spreadsheet-Type Presentation or Plan

The ACME Company
Project Profit and Loss Worksheet
Year Ended 31st December 1999
All figures in U.S. dollars—all salaries imaginary!

Name	Salary	Jan	Feb	Mar	Apr	May	Jun	Jul	Aug	Sep	Oct	Nov	Dec	Total
Salaries														
1 Overall Trailboss	100,000	8,333	8,333	8,333	8,333	8,333	8,333	8,333	8,333	8,333	8,333	8,333	8,333	100,000
2 Sales and Marketing trailb	47,250	4,410	4,410	4,410	4,410	4,410	4,410	4,410	4,410	4,410	4,410	4,410	4,410	52,920
3 Sales #1	18,000	1,680	1,680	1,680	1,680	1,680	1,680	1,680	1,680	1,680	1,680	1,680	1,680	20,160
4 Sales #2	18,000	1,680	1,680	1,680	1,680	1,680	1,680	1,680	1,680	1,680	1,680	1,680	1,680	20,160
5 Sales #3	15,000	1,400	1,400	1,400	1,400	1,400	1,400	1,400	1,400	1,400	1,400	1,400	1,400	16,800
6 Sales #4	66,000	6,160	6,160	6,160	6,160	6,160	6,160	6,160	6,160	6,160	6,160	6,160	6,160	73,920
7 Sales #5	66,000	6,160	6,160	6,160	6,160	6,160	6,160	6,160	6,160	6,160	6,160	6,160	6,160	73,920
8 Sales #5	66,000	6,160	6,160	6,160	6,160	6,160	6,160	6,160	6,160	6,160	6,160	6,160	6,160	73,920
9 Marketing	30,000	2,800	2,800	2,800	2,800	2,800	2,800	2,800	2,800	2,800	2,800	2,800	2,800	33,600
10 Trailboss	35,000	3,267	3,267	3,267	3,267	3,267	3,267	3,267	3,267	3,267	3,267	3,267	3,267	39,200
11 Facilities	16,000	1,493	1,493	1,493	1,493	1,493	1,493	1,493	1,493	1,493	1,493	1,493	1,493	19,227
12 Finance	18,000	1,680	1,680	1,680	1,680	1,680	1,680	1,680	1,680	1,680	1,680	1,680	1,680	20,160
13 Admin–Lisa	12,000	1,120	1,120	1,120	1,120	1,120	1,120	1,120	1,120	1,120	1,120	1,120	1,120	13,440
14 Admin–Maggie	12,000	1,120	1,120	1,120	1,120	1,120	1,120	1,120	1,120	1,120	1,120	1,120	1,120	13,440
15 Admin–Viki	10,000	933	933	933	933	933	933	933	933	933	933	933	933	11,200
16 Admin–new hire #1	11,000	1,027	1,027	1,027	1,027	1,027	1,027	1,027	1,027	1,027	1,027	1,027	1,027	12,320
17 Admin–new hire #2	12,000				1,120	1,120	1,120	1,120	1,120	1,120	1,120	1,120	1,120	10,080
18 Admin–new hire #3	12,000				1,120	1,120	1,120	1,120	1,120	1,120	1,120	1,120	1,120	10,080
19 HR	18,000	1,680	1,680	1,680	1,680	1,680	1,680	1,680	1,680	1,680	1,680	1,680	1,680	20,160
20 HR–part-time	10,000	933	933	933	933	933	933	933	933	933	933	933	933	11,200
21 Product delivery trailboss	52,000	4,853	4,853	4,853	4,853	4,853	4,853	4,853	4,853	4,853	4,853	4,853	4,853	58,240
22 Staff #1	43,680	4,077	4,077	4,077	4,077	4,077	4,077	4,077	4,077	4,077	4,077	4,077	4,077	48,922
23 Staff #2	50,400	4,200	4,200	4,200	4,200	4,200	4,200	4,200	4,200	4,200	4,200	4,200	4,200	50,400
24 Staff #3	12 dpm	3,600	3,600	3,600	3,600	3,600	3,600	3,600	3,600	3,600	3,600	3,600	3,600	43,200
25 Staff #4	43,680	4,077	4,077	4,077	4,077	4,077	4,077	4,077	4,077	4,077	4,077	4,077	4,077	48,922
26 Staff #5	40,000	3,733	3,733	3,733	3,733	3,733	3,733	3,733	3,733	3,733	3,733	3,733	3,733	44,800
27 Staff #6	33,000	3,080	3,080	3,080	3,080	3,080	3,080	3,080	3,080	3,080	3,080	3,080	3,080	36,960
28 Staff #7	44,000	4,107	4,107	4,107	4,107	4,107	4,107	4,107	4,107	4,107	4,107	4,107	4,107	49,280
29 Staff #8	40,000	3,733	3,733	3,733	3,733	3,733	3,733	3,733	3,733	3,733	3,733	3,733	3,733	44,800
30 Staff #9	33,000	3,080	3,080	3,080	3,080	3,080	3,080	3,080	3,080	3,080	3,080	3,080	3,080	36,960
31 Contractor	40,000	3,733	3,733	3,733	3,733	3,733	3,733	3,733	3,733	3,733	3,733	3,733	3,733	44,800
32 Staff #10	45,000					4,200	4,200	4,200	4,200	4,200	4,200	4,200	4,200	33,600
33 Staff #11	35,000					3,267	3,267	3,267	3,267	3,267	3,267	3,267	3,267	26,133
34 Staff #12	44,000								4,107	4,107	4,107	4,107	4,107	20,533
35 Staff #13	35,000								3,267	3,267	3,267	3,267	3,267	16,333
36 Staff #14	44,000								4,107	4,107	4,107	4,107	4,107	20,533
37 Staff #15	35,000								3,267	3,267	3,267	3,267	3,267	16,333
38 Staff #16	44,000								4,107	4,107	4,107	4,107	4,107	20,533
39 Staff #17	35,000											3,267	3,267	5,533
40 Staff #18	44,000											4,107	4,107	8,213
41 Trailboss	45,000	4,200	4,200	4,200	4,200	4,200	4,200	4,200	4,200	4,200	4,200	4,200	4,200	50,400
42 Product development #1	22,000	2,053	2,053	2,053	2,053	2,053	2,053	2,053	2,053	2,053	2,053	2,053	2,053	24,640
43 Product development #2	22,000	2,053	2,053	2,053	2,053	2,053	2,053	2,053	2,053	2,053	2,053	2,053	2,053	24,640
44 Q/A	15,000	1,400	1,400	1,400	1,400	1,400	1,400	1,400	1,400	1,400	1,400	1,400	1,400	16,800
45 IS #1	28,000	2,613	2,613	2,613	2,613	2,613	2,613	2,613	2,613	2,613	2,613	2,613	2,613	31,360
46 IS #2	45,000	4,200	4,200	4,200	4,200	4,200	4,200	4,200	4,200	4,200	4,200	4,200	4,200	50,400
47 IS #3	45,001	4,200	4,200	4,200	4,200	4,200	4,200	4,200	4,200	4,200	4,200	4,200	4,200	50,401
		115,030	115,030	115,030	117,270	124,737	124,924	124,924	143,777	143,777	143,777	151,150	151,050	1,570,578

Table 19.2 (continued)

Income														
Number of widgets		12	12	12	12	12	12	12	12	12	12	12	12	
Widget income		150,000	120,000	120,000	240,000	210,000	180,000	170,000	185,000	215,000	250,000	250,000	90,000	
Widget Mark ii's														
No. of Units		5	10	15	25	25	25	30	30	30	35	35	35	300
Average price (inlcuding training income)	1,985	9,925	19,850	29,775	49,625	49,625	49,625	59,550	59,550	69,475	69,475	69,475	69,475	595,500
Total Income		160,000	139,850	149,775	289,625	259,625	229,625	229,550	244,550	274,550	319,475	319,475	159,475	2,775,575
Expenses														
Director's fees		500	500	500	500	500	500	500	500	500	500	500	500	6,000
Staff costs		115,030	115,030	115,030	117,270	124,737	124,924	124,924	143,777	143,777	143,777	151,150	151,150	1,570,578
Telephone		5,500	5,500	5,500	5,500	5,500	5,500	5,500	5,500	5,500	5,500	5,500	5,500	66,000
Domestic motor and travel		4,000	4,000	4,000	4,000	4,000	4,000	4,000	4,000	4,000	4,000	4,000	4,000	48,000
International travel		3,000	3,000	3,000	3,000	3,000	3,000	3,000	3,000	3,000	3,000	3,000	3,000	36,000
Postage (inc. mailshots)		1,000	1,000	1,000	1,000	1,000	1,000	1,000	1,000	1,000	1,000	1,000	1,000	12,000
Rent		2,650	2,650	2,650	2,650	2,650	2,650	2,650	2,650	2,650	2,650	2,650	2,650	31,800
Municipal taxes		1,250	1,250	1,250	1,250	1,250	1,250	1,250	1,250	1,250	1,250	1,250	1,250	15,000
Stationery		3,000	3,000	3,000	3,000	3,000	3,000	3,000	3,000	3,000	3,000	3,000	3,000	36,000
Computer supplies		1,500	1,500	1,500	1,500	1,500	1,500	1,500	1,500	1,500	1,500	1,500	1,500	18,000
Training our people (per hour)	1,500				7,800	7,800	7,800	7,800	7,800	7,800	7,800	7,800	7,800	70,200
Leasing		3,000	3,000	3,000	3,000	3,000	3,000	3,000	3,000	3,000	3,000	3,000	3,000	36,000
Advertising (inc. recruitment)		1,000	10,000	1,000	1,000	10,000	1,000	1,000	1,000	10,000	1,000	1,000	1,000	39,000
Marketing collateral		1,000	1,000	1,000	1,000	1,000	1,000	1,000	1,000	1,000	1,000	1,000	1,000	12,000
Other markeing events				15,000						15,000				30,000
Web costs		1,000	1,000	1,000	1,000	1,000	1,000	1,000	1,000	1,000	1,000	1,000	1,000	12,000
Legal fees		2,000	2,000	2,000	2,000	2,000	2,000	2,000	2,000	2,000	2,000	2,000	2,000	24,000
Insurance		500	500	500	500	500	500	500	500	500	500	500	500	6,000
Facilities rent		1,500	1,500	1,500	1,500	1,500	1,500	1,500	1,500	1,500	1,500	1,500	1,500	18,000
Light and heat		500	500	500	500	500	500	500	500	500	500	500	500	6,000
Repairs and renewals		1,500	1,500	1,500	1,500	1,500	1,500	1,500	1,500	1,500	1,500	1,500	1,500	18,000
Pension					2,932	3,118	3,123	3,123	3,594	3,594	3,594	3,779	3,779	30,637
Software support		2,500	2,500	6,000	6,000	6,000	6,000	6,000	6,000	6,000	6,000	6,000	6,000	61,500
Audit				7,500			2,500							10,000
U.S. support													1,000	1,000
NT server			30,000	10,000	10,000			10,000						60,000
Software licenses		3,300	3,300	3,300	3,300	3,300	3,300	3,300	3,300	3,300	3,300	3,300	3,300	39,600
Telephone system				21,000										21,000
Disaster recovery maintenance		250	250	250	250	250	250	250	250	250	250	250	250	3,000
Miscellaneous		500	500	500	500	500	500	500	500	500	500	500	500	6,000
Hardware maintenance		500	500	500	500	500	500	500	500	500	500	500	500	6,000
Contingency		9,000	9,000	9,000	9,000	9,000	9,000	9,000	9,000	9,000	9,000	9,000	9,000	108,000
		165,480	225,480	197,980	191,952	198,605	192,297	199,797	209,121	233,121	209,121	216,679	217,679	
Profit/Loss		−5,480	−85,630	−48,205	97,673	61,020	37,328	29,753	35,429	41,429	110,354	102,796	−58,204	318,260

Table 19.3   Risk Analysis of Plan

	Risks	Likelihood	Impact	L x I	Action
1	Poor project management	2	3	6	Performance review Training Quality assurance Use of PSI
2	Under-resourcing	3	3	9	Verify targets against market data Advertise in January Sort dance cards
3	Managers get sick	1	2	2	
4	Over-resourcing	2	2	4	
5	Staff get sick	2	3	6	Shadowing Medicals for new employees Sort any existing problems
6	Lack of expertise	2	3	6	Training and development Proper and timely appraisals
7	Office space blowout	1	1	1	
8	New competitors	1	2	2	
9	Revenues don't happen—forecast is wrong	2	3	6	Weekly monitoring and change control Financial and mgmt. reports Difference between sales and revenue targets
10	Staff leave	1	3	3	
11	Clients walk	1	3	3	
12	Unrealistic goals	2	3	6	Change control
13	Data security	3	3	9	Discuss on 7 Dec.
14	Brand fatigue	2	2	4	
15	Competition	3	2	6	Competitive analysis Monthly review Spies Audits on lost customers
16	Get product mgmt. wrong	3	2	6	Define role Get trail boss Market research
17	Cash flow	2	3	6	Keep on it
18	Market changes	1	3	3	
19	Recession hits	1	3	3	
20	New market distracts management	1	3	3	

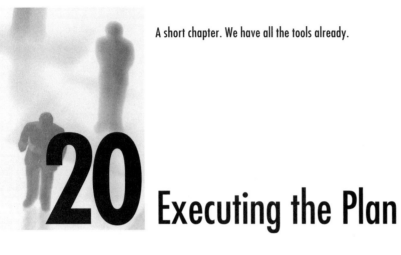

A short chapter. We have all the tools already.

20 Executing the Plan

Questions

? Q.1 Things are in meltdown. You can't quite put your finger on where it went wrong—you will, you hope, when it's all over—but revenues are falling, people are leaving, and it seems like no day brings good news. What do you do?

(a) Give up. Go get another job.

(b) Figure out where you are, figure out where you want to go, make a plan.

(c) Go out immediately to give a rousing speech to the troops to try to lift morale. Then consider your next move.

(d) Go out immediately and give a "don't work harder—work smarter" speech to the troops and then consider your next move.

? Q.2 Same scenario as previously. "But, but, but," you protest. I asked you the wrong question. If revenues are down then there are choices that I didn't give you in question 1. Here we go again. What do you do?

(a) Adopt a bunch of short-term measures to boost revenues.

(b) Adopt a bunch of short-term measures to reduce costs.

(c) Figure out where you are, figure out where you want to go, make a plan.

(d) Bring in consultants.

? Q.3   Same scenario as previously. So what's the real answer?

(a) Short-term revenue boosting and cost-cutting.

(b) Figure out where you are, figure out where you want to go, make a plan.

(c) Both of the above.

(d) Neither of the above.

Answers

Q.1
(a) 0 points: Come on—you're made of sterner stuff than that.
(b) 5 points: Yep.
(c) 0 points: A rousing speech at some stage certainly, but maybe let's have a little more plan first, so that the speech can have some context and people can feel there's a way forward.
(d) 0 points: Oh no. I saw it done once to disastrous effect. If they're not working smarter, guess who's responsible? You are.

Q.2
(a) 5 points: Yep.
(b) 5 points: Yep.
(c) 5 points: Yep.
(d) 0 points: Try the other three first.

Q.3
(a) 5 points: Certainly. If you don't do it, you could run out of cash.
(b) 5 points: "You can't drain the swamp," the old management saw goes, "if you're up to your ass in alligators." Ambitious swamp drainage measures are likely to be ended prematurely when an alligator grabs you. Alternatively, if all you do is kill alligators, you stay in the swamp. The key to this question is getting both the (a) activities and (b) activities rolling together. As we have tried to show, a serviceable plan can be put together very quickly—(b) activity. Then, build in your short-term, tactical measures—(a) activity—in the context of this longer term path.
(c) 5 points: Yep.
(d) 0 points: If you've got a better idea, I'd like to hear it.

Scores

15 points: Yes, but it wasn't too hard, was it?

1–14 points: Good enough.

0 points: Okay, maybe we're all tired. Anyway, the book is nearly finished.

Introduction

We've built the plan. Now we just need to execute it. (Just!)

Executing the plan

The lazy manager's weekly routine (Chapter 17) causes you to execute the plan. Apart from the OSR, there are two other indicators I find useful as an organization manager. One is to keep a PSI for the entire organization, considered as a single project. The other is to maintain the structured project management/step 4 assessments of people's capabilities.

PSI for the entire organization

Think of the OSR/OPI and PSI as a belt-and-braces approach to running your organization. The OSR/OPI are the detail status and health of the organization's projects. As we have seen, we update them weekly, and we should see a continuous upward trend in the OPI. Whenever it falls back, we know exactly where to look for trouble and what to do to fix it.

The PSI double checks this. It ensures that the places we are spending our time are indeed the right places. The PSI should also trend upward over time.

Step 4 assessments

Keep these at hand and look at them every day. Ensure that the people who report to you are getting the right level of attention, support, and mentoring from you.

User assistance

Table I (in the color section of this book) shows all of these indicators gathered in one place. The OSR/OPI readings are at the top; next come the PSI readings; and finally come the step 4 assignments. Think of Table I as your instrument panel as you run your organization.

PART FOUR
So Why Do Things Go Wrong?

In Part Four, the book shows you the traps you can fall into—if you're not careful. Chapter 21 does this for projects; Chapter 22 does it for organizations.

So if it's all as easy as we've said, why is it that so many projects go wrong? Here — by telling a bunch of war stories — we try to unearth some of the more common errors.

21

Why Do Projects Go Wrong?

Questions

❓ Q.1 If you follow all the guidelines in this book, then everybody will be happy all the time. True or false?

(a) True—if you follow *all* the guidelines.

(b) False.

(c) Dunno. I suspect it's a trick question.

(d) False. But my projects should run better.

❓ Q.2 The plan you wrote at the beginning of the project has become out-dated due to the unfolding of the project. Should you update it and, if so, how often?

(a) Yes—once a month.

(b) Yes—once more.

(c) No—everybody knows what needs to be done.

(d) No. You only did it to keep the standards department happy.

❓ Q.3 In choosing project managers, the things to look out for are:

(a) Charismatic personality.

(b) Attention to detail.

(c) Conscientious about keeping people informed.

(d) Assertive personality.

Answers

Q.1

(a) 0 points: "Everybody will be happy all the time"? Are you kidding?

(b) 5 points: Yes, the statement, as phrased, is false.

(c) 3 points: Perhaps it was something of a trick question. I was just trying to see if you were awake.

(d) 5 points: They should. Absolutely!

Q.2

(a) 5 points: This would be my preferred answer.

(b) 3 points: If this was all I was going to get, I'd settle for it.

(c) 0 points: There's an old saying that goes "if you don't have it in writing, you don't have it." This is a case in point.

(d) 0 points: At this stage in our relationship, I guess I give you this answer just to make you happy, and you pick it just to irritate me!

Q.3

(a) 0 points: Not necessarily, I would say.

(b) 5 points: For me, yes.

(c) 5 points: And this.

(d) 0 points: Can't always judge a book by its cover.

Scores

11–15 points: I think these questions are pretty straightforward, don't you?

1–10 points: Okay. A creditable attempt.

0 points: Let's just press on and read the chapter, shall we?

Introduction

Whether it looks it or not, a lot of thought went into the structure of this book and the arrangement of its chapters. Nowhere was this more true than with this chapter and Chapter 22. At first glance, it seemed obvious: I should put the "Why do things go wrong?" stuff at the beginning and then spend the rest of the book showing how use of the methods described in the book cause things *not* to go wrong. Among other things then, the book would close on a positive note—the proverbial happy ending.

However, the most obvious solution isn't always the best. While none of the things we've described in this book is rocket science, for reasons that I explore shortly, people very often don't *do* these things. Realizing this, it occurred to me that it would be better to end the book with a cautionary tale—or rather, a heap of cautionary tales. These might get remembered where some of the more cheery stuff might not—and in being remembered, they might cause the person doing the remembering to think twice before taking a path that could end up in tears. So, we end on the notes that follow. Some of the stories are happy, some not so; all are realistic descriptions of what the project management gods can do to you if you either play ball with them or try to mess with them.

So why do projects go wrong?

In my experience, projects fail for one of three reasons:

- People believe that projects are basically just a roll of dice and that there is nothing you can do to increase your chances of success. In terms of the terminology in this book, they are ignorant of the 10 steps.

- This is a variation of the first one. People know about the 10 steps—or some equivalent set of things—but they don't apply them because, somewhere deep down, *they don't actually believe that these things can make a difference.*

- People know about the 10 steps, but they look for a short-cut. Implicitly, they are thinking "maybe there are some things I don't have to do," ignoring the fact that the 10 steps are already a minimal set and can't be tightened any further without jeopardizing the project.

Often, with a particular project manager, one can only speculate as to which one of these sins they fell victim to. Also, it is less useful to do this than it is to examine the story of the project and to determine which of the following caused the project to go the way it did:

- Decisions;
- Actions;
- Responses to incidents.

The rest of this chapter does that with a series of cautionary tales—some about good projects, some about bad ones. The stories are designed to show the key issues that led to success or failure and these issues are flagged thus (step 7) with a reference to which of the steps was being used at that time.

I have chosen to do things this way because it is one thing to say that "projects fail if they don't have a well-defined goal." This is a bit like saying that a particular medical condition is life-threatening. It is quite a different—and, in my opinion, a much more useful—thing to say that "these are the symptoms of that condition." It is not possible to describe all of the particular sets of circumstances that make for successful or failed projects. However, I believe that the same *types* of things get done over and over again. The stories that follow are told not for their intrinsic interest, but actually for the opposite—their ordinariness.

If, in reading them, you come across something that strikes a chord, then look more closely. Maybe your project has that particular virtue or is suffering from this particular symptom. And maybe that is good news, or maybe—depending on the symptom—it's not good news at all.

A good exercise might be to write a little essay like this about one of your own projects, using the 10 steps as the basis for the "plot points" in your story. There are all sorts of interesting things that might emerge from such an exercise.

The first-time project manager's tale

One of the first projects I ever worked on had one deliverable (step 1). That deliverable was a magnetic tape—anyone remember those things, apart from me? While the processing that was going to go into the files on the tape was quite complex, the deliverable itself was very straightforward. The project would end when we wrote our tape and shipped it to another location, and they were able to read it and perform some further processing on it. I was working in a university at the time, and this project was to process the admissions to the university that year. There was a fixed deadline. Failure would mean people not getting places in the university or not getting the course of their choice or being lost somewhere in the processing. People get on prime-time news for smaller foul-ups than this. That was a television appearance I had no desire to make!

In a sense this was the best kind of project—a one-person one. I was both project manager and team (steps 3, 4, 6).

I didn't know anything about project management then. However, I did make lists of things that needed to get done (step 2). If one was being grand, one might call them plans. In reality they were giant to-do lists.

The project eventually completed and the tape shipped after a final session that began at 9 A.M. on one day and finished at 10 P.M. on the next day—a total stretch of 37 hours. It was the first and only time I've worked through the night. (It was also the first and only time I smoked cigarettes—to try and keep myself awake! Mary O'Riordan, who worked with me, provided the cigarettes. She has since given up the habit.) Though I didn't understand the significance of it at the time, this was where I found my contingency [step 5(a)].

Whenever anybody asked me how it was going, I told them (1) that I believed the project would work out and (2) what the actual status was at that point in time [steps 5(b), 7, 8]. The latter was done using objective project measures like "It's fine—no problem!" or "We've got *big* problems" or other similar phrases.

The project worked out successfully, and I didn't end up on TV—a happy outcome for all concerned.

A cautionary tale #1

I got my first big break in project management after the purge that took place on this next project. Here's the story that led up to the purge.

I joined the project as a COBOL programmer. The project manager would hand me specs, and I would write code from them. After a couple of weeks of doing this, I was given a briefing by another of the team. Two things were interesting about this briefing. First, this person made comments about the project manager not understanding the project technically (his phrasing was considerably less tactful than that which I just used). Second, he described to us a system (step 1) that would have terminals in ports all over southeast Asia and that would track vessel and container traffic. What this had to do with the routines I was writing, I failed completely to see. There was no plan. Not even a pretense at one (step 2).

There were two project managers, the one with the title and the one who had done the briefing and who thought that the one with the title was an idiot (step 3).

So, what of step 4—assigning people to jobs? Sure, people were assigned to, and worked on, things!

Contingency—step 5(a)? Well, when the excrement hit the ventilating device, what was done was that the project was renegotiated by the software company (for whom I worked) and the client.

Manage expectations—step 5(b)? Hardly. The fact that the project was off the rails came like a bolt out of the blue and was a huge surprise to everybody concerned.

Leadership styles—step 6? Both of the leaders (!) had different leadership styles.

There was no plan to monitor against (step 7), but there *was* weekly status reporting (step 8). (How is that possible, I ask myself.) I never saw the status reports, but one can only wonder at the kinds of days at the beach that were going on in them.

The purge, when it came, was not nice. Neither the project manager nor the man who thought the project manager was an idiot survived it. Looking back on it now, I am staggered that anybody got to run things like that ever.

The small software project manager's tale

Just to clarify the title—it was a small software project, not a small project manager! I ran a project (step 3) years ago to develop a software product. The environment was C/UNIX. (Not that it matters—I just threw that in for the techies among you!)

We wrote a requirements document and an HLD. These were reviewed and signed off by the powers that be (step 1). When changes occurred to either of these documents, as the project proceeded, we noted the changes in a series of change pages attached to each of the documents (step 1 again).

We did a plan (step 2, 4) and estimated the project two different ways, one using bottom-up estimating, the other using COCOMO, described in *Software Engineering Economics* by Barry Boehm [7]. The COCOMO estimate came out three times bigger than the other one, so we threw it away. (This is not to rubbish COCOMO. It had come out 100% accurate for me on a previous project, but on this occasion, we knew marketing wouldn't like the answer, so we—reluctantly—discarded the COCOMO estimate.)

(Just as an aside, note that the only estimating method we've described in this book is bottom-up estimating. In my opinion, it's the only method that I would have any confidence in—especially for software projects. If you want to see a good review of estimating methods in general, look at reference [7].)

The plan had hidden contingency in it [Step 5(a)]. It was hidden because if the powers that be had known about it, they would have whipped it out instantly. We told everybody when they could expect delivery of the product, and we successfully defended ourselves against any attempt to get us to shorten the deadline.

I did my usual job of managing the souls who worked on the project—(step 6). Depending on whom you talk to, they would probably describe my leadership style as ranging on a scale anywhere from very competent to wildly incompetent.

The plan was updated as we went along (step 7), and status reports were issued weekly (step 8).

We came in on time and on budget. As a result we—and particularly me—got to play the game again. This time, however, the game—and the stakes—were much higher.

A cautionary tale #2

In the early 1980s, the company I worked for set out to develop a range of machines consisting of a laptop computer, a desktop machine, and a mail server. This was a year before the launch of the IBM PC. Office automation was the fad at the time. Your laptop computer would be your office, and when you were out of the office, you could call the mail server from say, your hotel room, and download your e-mail. Such ideas are fairly passé now—at the time they were revolutionary.

The project was under way by the time I joined. Coding was in progress. Because of my success on the previous project, I was brought in to lead (step 3) the entire software development team—approximately 40 people consisting of operating system, applications (e.g., word processor, spreadsheet, diary), and communications groups.

(Again, by way of aside, I like to think that I came onto this project just as a small piece of the history of the computer industry was being made. The techies had to choose an operating system for the machine. The operating system group would then port it to the hardware that was under development. There were two contenders—something called MS-DOS and a vastly technically superior —multitasking, multiprocessing, all singing, all dancing—system called concurrent CPM (CCPM). Yes, you've guessed it—we chose the latter; in doing so, we probably put the first nail in the coffin that would eventually see us *not* becoming Compaq! Let me deal briefly with the rest of the nails!)

There was a spec. (step 1) that was long outdated by the time I arrived on the scene. There was a plan (steps 2 and 4) that was in a similar state. Nobody could tell me definitively what the scope of the project was.

The deadline was the date of the company's annual sales conference when the entire product line would be launched (step 5). There was an air about the place that anybody who questioned our ability to meet the deadline was being disloyal, in some way. It was a subtle but very invasive pressure.

Because of the rapid ramp-up in staff and new people continuously joining the project, the use of the correct leadership style (step 6) became almost impossible to gauge. Status tracking (step 7) was meaningless, since there was no plan, and so deadlines sailed by—a bit like all those icebergs the *Titanic* didn't hit, before it finally connected. There was some status reporting (step 8), but again, this had to be almost meaningless without a plan. The status reporting that was beamed out was always upbeat—again, the subtle pressure to only report good news. Yet, as the sales conference approached, the scope of the project continuously shrank until finally, only the laptop was going to be demonstrated.

In the end we probably ended up with a prototype of the laptop. About the same time, the IBM PC running MS-DOS came on the market. It was all too much. We gave up.

You might argue that this was a project that failed because of a technical error—the choice of operating system. I would disagree. I believe we got the scope of the project wrong. Part of the scope should have been to figure out what we planned to do about Big Blue. You may argue that this analysis uses too much hindsight. Perhaps. However, if you're not prepared to accept that argument, what about this: Assuming that we had shown ourselves capable of running a project that successfully gave birth to a laptop running CCPM, it would have been a relatively modest task for us to run a subsequent project to give birth to an MS-DOS laptop. It was our inability to do the former, with all the attendant financial loss, that caused us to have to pass on the latter.

The larger software project manager's tale

The project was about 20 people, and I was the leader (step 3). We had a very fraught time getting the requirements and design done. The chief designer was fired during the design phase. We used up 36% of the entire elapsed time getting the requirements and design complete and signed off (step 1). Strict change control was enforced (step 1, again). These two things—holding our fire until the design was agreed upon and strict change control thereafter—were the keys to this project's success.

There was a plan, built on detail, that included contingency [steps 2, 4, 5(a)]. The customer wanted us to meet a deadline that we believed to be impossible. We had told the customer as much [step 5(b)]. We had told him while we would give his date a try, we could reach, and would be prepared to guarantee, a date two months after his desired date. He accepted this. Note that this is not accepting an impossible mission. As part of giving it a try, there was no implication that we would work insane hours. Whenever the customer made noises in that direction, we made it clear that was an internal issue for us, and was/should be none of his concern. We told him of Tom DeMarco's book, *The Deadline* [11], which states that extended overtime is a productivity *reduction* tactic.

Again, the leadership style was mine, with all its eccentricities (step 6). Monitoring against the plan was done religiously every day (step 7); status reporting was weekly and non-day-at-the-beach (step 8).

Result? The project was indeed impossible within the desired time frame. However, the customer was never under any illusion otherwise. The status report contained three lines that read:

- Desired delivery date: His date;

- Committed delivery date: Our date (two months after his date);

- Current delivery date: What the delivery date was at that point in the project.

We met the committed delivery date. The product shipped on time and within budget, and for three months after it shipped, the product was in use and no bugs were reported in it.

We even had time to do a (really comprehensive) postmortem (step 10) on the project.

A final cautionary tale

The plan (steps 2, 4) said that the project would last two years. There was no contingency in the plan [Step 5(a)]. The requirements and design phases were planned to last for six months.

When the six months were up, the requirements were complete, but the design wasn't (step 1). The project leader made the decision that the development phase would have to begin. If it didn't, he reasoned, the project would surely run late.

The project leader was experienced with a good use of leadership styles (steps 3 and 6). There was no real monitoring against the plan, and status reporting was every six months (steps 7 and 8). (In my opinion, for "every six months" you can effectively read "nonexistent.")

After a further year (i.e., 18 months into the project), the following was the situation:

- Bits of the product existed—some well-tested, some in prototype form.

- Bits were under development.

- Bits had not yet been specified or designed.

- Bits that had already been developed were being reworked.

The remedial action—note that this is a project rescue—taken was to do the following:

1. Assess precisely what did and didn't exist.

2. For those things that did exist, assess the state they were in.

3. Specify precisely what the final objective was (step 1).

4. Build a plan [steps 2, 4, 5(a), 5(b)]. Two points to note about the plan: (1) among the first activities in the plan were the specification and design of the remaining pieces; and (2) by involving all of the project participants in the replanning exercise, expectations were managed very precisely.

5. The same project leader continued the project (steps 3 and 6).

6. Monitoring against the plan was made one of the project leader's key activities (step 7).

7. Monthly status reports were introduced (step 8). (While it wasn't ideal, it was better than what had preceded it.)

8. The project completed an additional six months after its original two-year deadline.

Epilogue

So what have we seen at the end of all of this? We have seen that there are perhaps infinitely many ways in which the 10 steps can either be adhered to or violated. There is no variety, however, in the results that occur in both cases.

Violate one or more of our principles and you will be punished. I can't say it plainer than that.

So if it's still all as easy as we've said, why is it that not just projects, but whole organizations can go off the rails? And can the techniques we've talked about stop this from happening?

22 Why Do Organizations Go Wrong?

Questions

? Q.1 The organization is happy. There's a buzz in the air. Things are happening according to plan. Does this mean:

(a) There's a huge disaster just around the corner.

(b) You've deluded yourself—you're not reading the signs right.

(c) That you don't know what it means.

(d) Things are actually looking good—for once.

? Q.2 In designing new products for your organization, the people who will have the most valuable input to give to the design process are:

(a) Marketing.

(b) Design people.

(c) Customers.

(d) Management.

❢ Q.3 A particular month turns out to be quite different (for "different" read "worse") than what the plan predicted. How long before you take action?

(a) Don't wait—take it now.

(b) Wait another month to see if the reading is still the same. If it is, take action.

(c) Wait a quarter and see if the reading is the same. Then take action.

(d) Dunno. Haven't given me enough material to go on in the question.

Answers

Q.1

(a) 4 points: As we've said earlier, a healthy insecurity is not necessarily a bad thing.

(b) 2 points: Always a possibility, but if things are happening according to plan, then that's a good sign.

(c) 0 points: No. Again, things going according to plan is an objective measure of progress.

(d) 5 points: Provided you maintain the healthy insecurity, I'd say "Why not?"

Q.2

(a) 3 points: Their input will be valuable, but it won't be the most valuable.

(b) 3 points: Similarly.

(c) 5 points: Of course.

(d) 2 points: 2 points on the basis that, in general, it's probably less valid than that of the marketing or design people.

Q.3

(a) 3 points: A lot to be said for it, but it might be too soon.

(b) 5 points: For me, yes.

(c) 0 points: For me, this is almost definitely too long.

(d) 3 points: Maybe not, but I think your answer should either have been (a) or (b).

Scores

15 points: Hard to get full marks here.

5–14 points: Yes, some of these are a matter of style.

How to Run Successful High-Tech Project-Based Organizations

0–4 points: We obviously approach things differently.

Introduction

My contention would be that organizations go wrong for exactly the same reasons that projects do. (The list is given in Chapter 1.) However, for me to just go on saying this is perhaps less useful than adopting a different approach.

Let's say we find somebody who has studied organizations and the reasons they go wrong. Then, let's take this person's findings, map them into the things we have been talking about, and see what emerges.

I have referred already to Eileen Shapiro's book *The Seven Deadly Sins of Business—Freeing the Corporate Mind from Doom-Loop Thinking* [10]. In this book, Shapiro proposes seven reasons why organizations get themselves into a mess. What I propose to do here is the following:

1. Show that each of these seven reasons is basically nothing more than a breach of one or more of the 10 steps.

2. Show that by applying the 10 steps, you increase your chances of not committing one or more of Shapiro's "seven sins."

The rest of this chapter is divided into seven sections, covering each of Shapiro's "sins."

Terrific plans

Shapiro describes this problem as "Aggressive targets are set without sufficient overall guidance to help people with the 'how's.' Guidance on the 'how's' needn't be complex or exhaustive, but it does need to provide more direction than specific numerical goals or expansive vision statements alone."

In our terminology, the problem here is that people do one of the following.

- Set a goal but no plan of how to get there;

- Set a goal, build a sort of a plan, but a plan that contains only some numeric targets, and in particular, omits any of the intangible or people-related issues that we talked about in Part One.

In the 10 steps, the goal and the plan to get there are inseparable. The plan cannot take place without the goal. However, once the goal is identified, the plan flows logically from the goal. The plan also helps to tighten the definition of the goal. In addition, by trying to identify the best possible outcome, we end up trying to find win conditions for all of the project stakeholders. In summary, steps 1–5 are a way of ensuring that we don't become guilty of this first organizational "sin."

Outstanding products

This can be put simply as building products that nobody wants. In our terminology, it's a failure to describe the goal of the project correctly. At the risk of stating the blindingly obvious, the customers for whom we make our products are one of the stakeholders in setting the goal. If creating happy customers is not a goal of your organization, then one would have to wonder what you are doing in business.

In setting the goal of our project, in establishing the best possible outcome—the and-they-all-lived-happily-ever-after outcome—win conditions for all the stakeholders are key. If, in building products, we omit the most key stakeholder of all—the customer—then the chances of us building products they would want have to be reasonably remote.

On the other hand, inclusion of all of the stakeholders in step 1 will ensure that we don't commit the second organizational "sin."

Play to win

When you build your organizational plan or strategy, you make a prediction of how you believe the world is going to behave. Sometimes (sometimes!), the world subsequently behaves differently from the way you had predicted. If this happens to you, then this problem is about whether you continue to play the old game, or rather that you realize things have changed and try to figure out a new way of going forward. Scott Peck in *The Road Less Traveled*

[12] gives a nice definition of insanity as "doing the same thing over and over again and expecting different results."

If you continue to play the old game, then you do indeed breach the 10 steps. You breach step 9 which says that you don't just plan once, and then take a giant jump to the end. Rather you are constantly planning and doing, planning and doing.

If you set out believing you were heading for a certain goal along a certain track, and you now find that the path you are taking is nothing like what you expected, then this means that you will most likely end up in a different place (goal) from what you expected. To fix this you must mount a sort of ongoing rescue of your project to return it to the place you believe it should be heading.

One of the reasons you have a plan in the first place is to give you some sort of frame of reference when you go out into the uncharted future. You can't *know* what it will actually be like, but you can predict what you expect it to be like. You can then use this prediction as your benchmark. If things veer too widely from your benchmark, you can rework your plan to take it in a new direction that is more in keeping with where you want to end up.

Turbo-charged employees

This is about not "training"—in the broadest sense of the word —employees to maximize both their own potential and their contribution to the organization. Training here includes formal training, on-the-job training, mentoring, and empowerment. This "sin" represents a breach of steps 4 and 6.

Because everything is changing so much, one of the things that has become evident to me over the last few years is the number of times you end up having to consider someone a trainee. This is often despite the fact that they may have a resume as long as your arm and many years of qualifications and experience. One of the results of this is that when you apply step 4, you may come to the realization that your particular project has a large number of trainee-type situations on it.

One way of dealing with this is just to grin and bear it. Among other things, this implies living with the micromanagement that such a situation implies.

An alternative approach is to try and put a sequence of jobs in place (step 2) that will essentially "train" that person to do the job you are asking them to do. For projects this sometimes isn't the most efficient way forward—the training may add an intolerable overhead to an already fragile project. On the other hand, if you are envisaging a series of projects, then such training may make total sense—and for *organizations*, such training almost always make sense, as it gives the organization a strength in depth that it may otherwise lack.

Workplace sizzle

This problem has to do with not giving the employees the right motivators. In my opinion, this goes back to a breach of step 1. It is a failure to get the goal right, to take account of all of the stakeholders and their win conditions. It is a failure to think that there might be any other goal to the project other than the one that sees certain financial indicators—revenue, profit, various rations—met. This is essentially the same problem as that identified above except with a different set of stakeholders neglected this time. The solution again, of course, is the inclusion of all the stakeholders in the discussions about project goal/vision.

Learning organization

The problem here is that organizations pay lip service to the notion of being a "learning organization." In reality, nothing could be further from the truth, and if the facts don't fit the theory, then the facts get changed!

This is a breach of step 7, where the recording of actual data takes place, and step 8 where progress of the project is reported on. It is also a breach of the philosophy underlying the 10 steps, which says that we recognize the following:

- That successful project management involves predicting the future;

- That one of the few ways we can improve our ability to predict the future is to record actual hard data, as opposed to rose-tinted impressions.

Thus, the keys to not falling into this particular trap are the following:

- Record what actually happens on the project ("actuals"), against what we predicted would happen ("estimates"). Despite what people say, it's mighty hard to argue with facts.

- Report status in the objective way we have described.

- Push that people *act* on the status report. This is particularly true if the news is bad. Watch for people trying to water down bad news in the hope that by the time it all falls apart, they'll have moved on to bigger and better things, and you can be left positioned in the gun sights, holding the baby—if you'll pardon the mixed metaphor.

Forward intelligence system

The issue here refers to whether the powers that be act on information, especially negative information, flowing up the chain. Also, more fundamentally, it refers to whether the organizational culture is such that people are prepared to be the bearers of bad news. This is a breach of step 8.

At the risk of sounding like a broken record, let us say it one more time: Good, bad, or indifferent, one of the project manager's jobs is to pass the status back to the other stakeholders. His or her job is twofold:

- To ensure that what gets passed is an accurate reflection of the health of the project;

- To ensure that the appropriate action gets taken upon receipt of this information.

Conclusion

The plan we build for our organization serves a number of purposes.

1. It gives us the clearest picture achievable of what we are dealing with, what we are trying to do, and most importantly, what the best possible outcome achievable is.

2. It stops us from committing to things that are not possible.

3. It is our best guess of what the future will be like. Thus, it acts as a direction finder and as an early-warning system. In a very real sense, it is our instrumentation to drive and guide the project.

From the first of these viewpoints, we have seen yet again the importance of stakeholder buy-in. Stakeholders will buy in if they feel that the successful completion of the project represents a win situation for them.

From the third of these viewpoints, should it happen that, as the project proceeds, we veer from the plan, then we ignore such warning signs at our peril. On the other hand, if we honestly try to understand why things are happening and to modify our goals where necessary and our plans constantly, then the completion of our plan should not represent a surprise to anybody.

Bibliography

This book directly refers to the following sources:

[1] O'Connell, Fergus, *How To Run Successful Projects II—The Silver Bullet*, Hemel Hempstead, England: Prentice Hall, 1996.

[2] DeMarco, Tom, and Timothy Lister, *Peopleware*, New York: Dorset House Publishing, 1987.

[3] Brooks, F. P., *The Mythical Man-Month*, Reading, MA: Addison-Wesley, 1975.

[4] Yourdon, Edward, *Death March*, New York: Prentice Hall, 1997.

[5] British Standards Institute, *Guide to Project Management* (BS 6079), London: 1996.

[6] Davenport, Thomas H., and Laurence Prusak, *Working Knowledge—How Organizations Manage What They Know*, Cambridge, MA: Harvard Business School Press, 1998.

[7] Boehm, Barry, *Software Engineering Economics*, Englewood Cliffs, NJ: Prentice Hall, 1981.

[8] Microsoft Corporation, *Cinemania*, 1994 edition.

[9] Humphrey, Watts, *Managing the Software Process*, Reading, MA: Addison-Wesley, 1989.

[10] Shapiro, Eileen, *The Seven Deadly Sins of Business—Freeing the Corporate Mind from Doom-Loop Thinking,* Oxford, England: Capstone, 1998.

[11] DeMarco, Tom, *The Deadline,* New York: Dorset House, 1997.

[12] Peck, M. Scott, *The Road Less Traveled,* Llandeilo, Wales, U.K.: Simon & Schuster, 1998.

Other references

Howard, Ron (director), *Apollo 13,* Los Angeles: Universal Studios, 1995. Motion picture. A project that goes wrong but ultimately has a happy ending. (Not too many of them, I think you'll agree.) Also some great lines (and advice), for example, "Let's work the problem, people—let's not make things worse by guessing."

Petroski, Henry, *To Engineer is Human: The Role of Failure in Successful Design*, New York: Random House, 1992. Petroski is a civil engineer but his advice on lessons learned could be applied to almost any field.

About the Author

Fergus O'Connell graduated with a first in mathematical physics from University College Cork. His 23 years of experience—20 of those in project management positions—cover commercial data processing, microprocessor-based office automation systems, computer networking, data communications, and telecommunications. He began his career in the Computer Centre of University College Cork and worked with companies such as CPT, ICL, and Retix before founding ETP in 1992. His experience covers projects in Australia, Britain, Denmark, Germany, Ireland, Luxembourg, Sweden, Switzerland, and the United States. He has taught project management courses on three continents.

Fergus is the author of the best-selling *How To Run Successful Projects II—The Silver Bullet* (Prentice Hall, 1996). In addition, he has written about project management for the *Sunday Business Post*, *Computer Weekly*, *DEC Computing*, and the *Wall Street Journal*. He has lectured on project management at University College Cork and Boston University and on television for the National Technological University.

He lives with his wife, son, daughter, three dogs, two horses, three ponies, and a donkey beside the River Barrow in Ireland. He is currently chairman and CEO of ETP.

Index

Recent Titles in the Artech House Computing Library

For further information on these and other Artech House titles,
including previously considered out-of-print books now available through
our In-Print-Forever® (IPF®) program, contact:

Artech House
685 Canton Street
Norwood, MA 02062
Phone: 781-769-9750
Fax: 781-769-6334
e-mail: artech@artechhouse.com

Artech House
46 Gillingham Street
London SW1V 1AH UK
Phone: +44 (0)20 7596-8750
Fax: +44 (0)20 7630-0166
e-mail: artech-uk@artechhouse.com

Find us on the World Wide Web at:
www.artechhouse.com